Too many of us, regardless of ou  Bible, are blind to the story of th trees. We fail to recognize how t together to tell one mega-story. and us.

Phil Vischer
Creator of Veggie Tales and What's in the Bible? video series

As a university professor on a Christian college campus, I can tell you that biblical illiteracy is on the rise. That's why the Bible Savvy series should be a prerequisite reading for everyone. Jim Nicodem puts the cookies on the bottom shelf by making the epic story of the biblical narrative understandable and accessible. The Bible Savvy series lays out the foundation and context for God's Word and then shows us in plain language how to apply the Bible's teachings to our lives step-by-step. It's phenomenal.

Les Parrott, PhD
Seattle Pacific University
Author of *You're Stronger Than You Think*

The compelling reality about the Bible is that it is full of fascinating details about God and His wise and redemptive oversight of the history of mankind. Unfortunately, the larger, more profound story often gets lost in the details. Like a master storyteller, Jim Nicodem takes us beyond the details and exposes the grand plot of Scripture. Jim's work in the Bible Savvy series will amaze many of us who have lived to master the details and will motivate all of us to stand in greater awe of the One who is navigating history to a good and glorious end.

Joseph M. Stowell
President, Cornerstone University

The Bible is one of the most precious possessions to a believer living in a restricted nation. I am constantly amazed by the hunger for biblical teaching expressed by those who face persecution daily. Their sacrificial passion should inspire us to rekindle our quest for biblical understanding. Jim Nicodem's Bible Savvy series is the kind of resource needed to reengage our hearts and minds with God's Word, and renew a hunger for God's truth on par with our persecuted brother and sisters.

> James E. Dau
> President, The Voice of the Martyrs

Jim has done a masterful job in the Bible Savvy series! In these four concise books, Jim marches with clarity and skill into topics that would be difficult to tackle in a seminary classroom, much less in an American living room. And rather than a monologue, these books create a dialog among the author, the reader, their small group, and the living Word of God. These practical, approachable resources provide foundational training that is greatly needed by nearly every small group and leader I encounter.

> Greg Bowman
> Coauthor of *Coaching Life-Changing Small Group Leaders*
> Past executive director of the Willow Creek Association

Reading the four books in the Bible Savvy series is like getting a Bible college education in a box! The Lord is calling our nation to a Bible reading revolution, and these books are an invitation to be part of it.

> Hal Seed
> Author of *The Bible Questions* and *The God Questions*
> Lead Pastor, New Song Community Church, Oceanside, California

Living in the land of the Bible is considered a privilege by many, but the real privilege is to let the Bible become alive through us, in whatever land we may live. In the Bible Savvy series, Jim Nicodem not only helps us to understand God's plan to save us, but also His desire to change and shape us through His Word and Spirit in order to be a light in this dark world.

> Rev. Azar Ajaj
> Vice President and lecturer, Nazareth Evangelical Theological Seminary

To ignite a love for the God's Word in others is the goal of any spiritual leader. Communicating God's Word is the most important of all. Pastor Jim's Bible Savvy series is the tool, the guide, and the process for worship leaders to go into deep spiritual places. His biblical scholarship, communicated with such creativity, is exactly what is needed in worship ministry today.

> Stan Endicott
> Slingshot group coach/mentor
> Worship Leader, Mariners Church, Irvine, California

Jim Nicodem leads one of America's finest churches. Jim knows how to communicate the truth of the Bible that brings historical knowledge with incredible practical application. The Bible Savvy series is the best I have ever seen. Your life and faith will be enhanced as you use and apply this material to your life.

> Jim Burns, PhD
> President, HomeWord
> Author of *Creating an Intimate Marriage* and
> *Confident Parenting*

Pastor Nicodem is like a championship caliber coach: he loves to teach, and he stresses that success comes from mastering the basics. The Bible Savvy series will help you correctly interpret the best Playbook ever written: the Bible. Understanding and applying its fundamentals (with the help of the Bible Savvy series) will lead one to the Ultimate Victory . . . eternity with Jesus.

> James Brown
> Host of *The NFL Today* on the CBS television network

JAMES L. NICODEM

Bible Savvy

Hear from the author by checking out the videos on the Bible Savvy Series with James Nicodem.

biblesavvy.com

MOODY
PUBLISHERS

Context

How to Understand the Bible

James L. Nicodem

MOODY PUBLISHERS

CHICAGO

All Scripture quotations are taken from the *Holy Bible, New International Version*®, NIV®. Copyright © 1973, 1978, 1984 by Biblica, Inc.™ Used by permission of Zondervan. All rights reserved worldwide.

Scripture quotations marked AMP are taken from *The Amplified Bible*. Copyright © 1965, 1987 by The Zondervan Corporation. *The Amplified New Testament* copyright © 1958, 1987 by The Lockman Foundation. Used by permission.

Published in association with the literary agency of Wolgemuth & Associates, Inc.

Edited by Jim Vincent
Interior design: Ragont Design
Cover design: Smartt Guys design
Cover image: Thomas Northcut

Library of Congress Cataloging-in-Publication Data

Nicodem, James L., 1956-
    Context : how to understand the Bible / James L. Nicodem.
       pages cm. — (The Bible savvy series)
    Includes bibliographical references.
    ISBN 978-0-8024-0635-4
    1. Bible—Introductions. I. Title.
    BS475.3.N53 2013
    220.6'1—dc23
                                                    2012047218

We hope you enjoy this book from Moody Publishers. Our goal is to provide high-quality, thought-provoking books and products that connect truth to your real needs and challenges. For more information on other books and products written and produced from a biblical perspective, go to www.moodypublishers.com or write to:

Moody Publishers
820 N. LaSalle Boulevard
Chicago, IL 60610

3 5 7 9 10 8 6 4 2

Printed in the United States of America

About the
Bible Savvy Series

I MET THE REAL ESTATE AGENT at my front
door and invited him in. My wife and I were about to put
our home on the market and I had called Jeff as a potential
representative. As he sat down at our dining room table and
opened his briefcase, I noticed a Bible perched on top of other
papers. I asked Jeff if he was a Bible reader and he replied that
he was just getting started. What had prompted his interest?
He'd recently come across a list in *Success, Inc.* magazine of
the most influential books recommended by business leaders.
The Bible had been the most frequently mentioned book on
the list. So, Jeff was going to give it a try.

My real estate agent isn't alone in his new interest in the
Bible. According to a recent survey, 91 percent of those who
have lately begun attending church were motivated to do so
by a desire to understand what the Bible has to say to their
lives.[1] That means nine of every ten visitors to church are in-
trigued by the Bible! But while they are curious about God's
Word, they're also a bit intimidated by it. The Bible is such
a daunting book, written in ancient times and addressed to

vastly different cultures. Is it really possible to draw relevant insights from it for our lives today? People are returning to church to find out.

Ironically, while an interest in Bible knowledge can be detected among those who are new to church, it seems to be on the wane among many veteran churchgoers. When my oldest daughter enrolled at a Christian college, the president of the school addressed parents on opening day. He told us that the Bible comprehension exams of each incoming class of freshmen show less and less knowledge of God's Word. And then he added: "These kids are growing up in *your* churches." Evidently, many churches are not doing a good job of teaching committed believers how to read, interpret, and apply the Bible.

The Bible Savvy series has been written to help a wide spectrum of Bible readers—from newbies to seasoned Bible study leaders—get their arms around God's Word. This multibook series covers four essential Bible-related topics that Moody Publishers has made available in one set as a comprehensive manual for understanding God's Word and putting it into practice. *Context* is the third of the four-book series.

An added bonus to the Bible Savvy series is the Study Guide that follows every chapter of each book. These questions for personal reflection and group discussion have been crafted by a team of small-groups experts. The Study Guide is also available online at biblesavvy.com and may be downloaded and used for personal study or reproduced for members of a small group.

Four Things You Must Know to
Get the Most out of God's Word

The four books of the Bible Savvy series will give you a grasp of the following topics, allowing God's Word to become a rich resource in your life:

1. *The storyline of the Bible.* The Bible is actually a compilation of sixty-six books that were written over a 1,500-year period. But amazingly there is one central storyline that holds everything together. You'll trace this storyline in *Epic* from Genesis to Revelation, learning how each of the sixty-six books contributes to the overall plot.

2. *The reliability of the Bible.* How did God communicate what He wanted to say through human authors? What are the evidences that the Bible is a supernatural book? How do we know that the *right* books made it into the Bible and that the *wrong* books were kept out of it? Isn't a text that was handcopied for hundreds of years bound to be filled with errors? *Foundation* will give you answers to questions

like these—because you won't get much out of the Bible until you're certain that you can trust it.

3. *How to understand the Bible.* People read all sorts of crazy things into the Bible, and have used it to support a wide variety of strange (and sometimes reprehensible) positions and activities. In *Context* you will learn the basic ground rules for accurately interpreting Scripture. (Yes, there are rules.)

4. *How to apply the Bible.* It's one thing to read the Bible, and it's another thing entirely to walk away from your reading with an application for your life. Even members of Bible study groups occasionally do a poor job of this. Participants leave these gatherings without a clear sense of how they're going to put God's Word into practice. *Walk* will equip you to become a Bible doer.

Do You Have Savvy?

The dictionary defines *savvy* as *practical know-how.* It is my hope and prayer that the Bible Savvy series will lead you into an experiential knowledge of God's Word that will transform your life.

Many people have contributed to my own love and understanding of the Bible over the years—as well as to the writing of this book. I owe a huge debt of gratitude to them.

Mom and Dad made God's Word central to our family life, encouraging my siblings and me to memorize big chunks of it.

When I got to high school, I was a bit turned off to church, but I started attending a youth ministry in a neighboring suburb that was led by Bill Hybels. (These were pre–Willow Creek Community Church days, when dinosaurs roamed the earth.) Bill had (and still has) an incredible ability to open the Bible, read a passage out loud, and then drive home its application to the lives of his listeners. After a year of hearing him teach God's Word in such a life-impacting way, I went away to college and decided to major in biblical studies.

Two professors (among many) fanned the flame of my love for the Bible during my college and seminary years. Dr. Gerry Hawthorne taught me Greek New Testament at Wheaton College, and there are thousands of men and women in ministry around the world today who still remember his simple-but-powerful class devotions. He'd put one verse on the chalkboard (remember chalk?) and then tease out its significance for our lives—often with tears in his eyes. Dr. D. A. Carson taught me the Bible at Trinity Evangelical Divinity School. His books (and occasional phone and email exchanges) continue to shape me today. I aspire to have even a quarter of his passion for God's Word!

After school, as I started out in youth ministry, I began listening to cassette tapes (same era as chalk) by Dr. John

MacArthur. John is internationally famous for his verse-by-verse teaching of Scripture. Although he is occasionally more adamant about certain doctrines than I am (we agree on the essentials), his love for the Bible is infectious. John has set the bar high for all pastors who want to faithfully teach their churches God's Word. As my ministry has continued, I have found other communicators who whet my appetite for Scripture—many of them through their books, some of them currently through their podcasts. Thank you Lee Strobel, Joe Stowell, John Ortberg, Mark Driscoll, Francis Chan, Tim Keller, and many others.

Today, my desire to get people into the Bible is fueled by the five thousand-plus eager learners whom I have the privilege of pastoring at Christ Community Church of St. Charles, Illinois, and its regional campuses. I am especially grateful for both the staff and volunteer leaders who oversee almost four hundred Community Groups that are studying God's Word. And one of those leaders, who writes incredible Bible curricula and teaches scores of Bible-hungry women, is my wife, Sue. Her devotion to Scripture is a constant inspiration to me.

Lastly, a special thanks to my faithful assistant, Angee Jenkins, who helped to edit my manuscript, track down footnotes, and protect my writing time; and to my agent, Andrew Wolgemuth, who found a great publisher in Moody to make the Bible Savvy series available to you.

*To watch Jim's introduction to Context,
scan this QR code with your smartphone or go to
www.biblesavvy.com/video/#context1.*

Contents

Foreword

THE BIBLE CLEARLY says, "There is no God." That's an exact quotation from the Bible. Of course, including a wee bit more of the context reverses one's understanding: "The fool says in his heart, 'There is no God'" (Psalm 14:1). Paying attention to the immediate context makes all the difference.

This example, of course, is too easy. Sometimes contexts reach beyond a verse or a paragraph or a chapter. Sometimes they extend to an entire biblical book or to an author like Paul—or even to the entire canon of Scripture. To be sensitive to the context demands alertness not only to words and sentences, but to the diverse literary forms of Scripture.

Now, some people are better readers than others. They instinctively uncover the plot of a narrative, listen carefully for the characterizations of people mentioned in the text, pick up on repeated topics, and think carefully about words. They may not know much about rules of interpretation; they are simply good readers. But *all* readers—better readers and poorer readers—will benefit from some introductory exposure to how literature *works*, including biblical literature. And which of us would not want to become better, more accurate, more attentive readers of God's most holy Word?

God in His wisdom has not only given us Scripture, but He has ordained that there be pastor/teachers in the church. Such pastors are more gifted than many others at understanding Scripture and explaining it to others. They have a peculiar function within the body: they are like stomachs that take in nourishment and distribute it to the rest of the body.

So think of Jim Nicodem as a stomach. As a pastor, what Jim does in this short book is something a little more and a little less than simply explain Scripture in order to nourish the body. Although he provides many examples that actually do explain this or that passage of Scripture, his purpose is to lay out, in straightforward, nontechnical language, many of the most important principles of interpretation. He does this so each person may know the foundational principles of biblical interpretation, and so understand many texts. In other words, Jim wants the church he serves, and many other churches, to be filled with men and women who will become better Bible readers. If you think your way carefully through this book, Jim's high goal will be amply realized.

D. A. CARSON, PhD
Research Professor of New Testament
Trinity Evangelical Divinity School
Author of *New Testament Commentary Survey*

Introduction:
Fitting the Pieces Together

JIGSAW PUZZLES are a popular holiday diversion in my home. After a big meal with family and friends, our guests will fan out into different rooms to read, talk, nap, or watch a ball game. But inevitably a card table will be set up in the living room, a lamp will be plugged in nearby for greater illumination, and the thousand pieces of a jigsaw puzzle are dumped out for assembly.

There are usually a few diehards in the group who stay at it from beginning to end. But almost everybody contributes at some point—grandparents, teenagers, ball game watchers on commercial breaks. It's irresistible. You can't stop at the table for even a minute without picking up a piece and trying to put it in its proper spot. And when our puzzles are completed, we coat their surfaces with a transparent glue (Mod Podge, if you're interested) and hang them on the walls of our downstairs playroom as decorations.

As a person who knows something about puzzles, I can tell you that an indispensable aid to putting one together is the top of the box that it comes in. That's where the picture is. The picture lets you know what your final product is supposed to look like. A giant cheeseburger? A bouquet of flowers? A Norman Rockwell painting? A panoramic view of the Grand Canyon?

More importantly, the picture gives you clues about where to place each puzzle piece that you hold in your hand. Is it blue? Then it's probably part of the sky in the upper right portion of the puzzle. Does it have letters on it? Then it must belong to the sign on the side of the building that's in the puzzle's center.

I would never try putting a puzzle together without looking at the box top. Any puzzle assembler needs to know the overall picture. Unfortunately, this is not how many people approach the Bible. They read it in bits and pieces, without reference to its big picture. They have no idea how it all fits together. They're unfamiliar with the larger context of a particular passage that they're looking at. And this makes it difficult to understand that passage correctly.

Context (the third book in the Bible Savvy series) will equip you to interpret God's Word with accuracy. The key to the process is understanding the Bible's big picture. We're going to look at that big picture from four vantage points. We'll be considering the Bible's historical, literary, theological, and immediate settings. Don't be intimidated by these four categories. You will fully understand what is meant by each and how they can help you better understand the Bible by the time you're done reading the following pages.

{ 1 }
The Historical Setting

I WAS A BIBLICAL STUDIES major in college. One of my favorite professors taught me Old Testament and Hebrew. He was a very dignified, articulate, God-fearing man. He kind of reminded me of an ancient prophet. One Sunday I stopped by his house to drop something off and his wife was getting their six-year-old son, Scotty, ready for church in another room.

In the middle of my conversation with this professor, we heard Scotty scream at the top of his lungs: "I don't want to go to church! You can't make me go to church! I HATE CHURCH!!" The face of my very dignified, articulate, God-fearing professor turned beet-red with embarrassment. But he very quietly said to me: "You must understand the *context* of that outburst. You see, Scotty has just been pulled from the sandbox."

Ahhh! "You must understand the context." That also happens to be the most important rule for interpreting the Bible. *You must understand the context.* Have you ever heard a skeptic complain, "Oh, people can make the Bible say whatever they want it to say"? That skeptic is absolutely right. People *can* make the Bible say whatever they want it to say—*if* they take Bible verses out of context. But that's a violation of the number one ground rule for interpreting the Bible.

There are ground rules for interpreting the Bible? Yes, there are ground rules for interpreting *any* piece of serious writing, whether it's the Bible, Shakespeare's plays, Robert Frost's poems, or Jane Austen's novels. Interpreting great literature requires ground rules. The ground rules for interpreting the Bible are called *hermeneutics.*

Herman who? *Hermeneutics* is a Greek word. If you know your Greek mythology, you probably recall that Hermes was the messenger god. He was responsible for conveying information from the gods to humans. So, hermeneutics refers to the ground rules that must be followed in order to ensure that the Word of God, the Bible, is accurately understood by us.

Context is really just a short course in hermeneutics. No matter what your current level of Bible understanding, you need hermeneutics. If you're not yet a Bible reader because you're put off by a book that's set in cultures so vastly different from your own, you need hermeneutics. If you regularly read the Bible but come across passages that leave you asking, "What in the world does this mean?" you need hermeneutics. If you want to hear God speak to you through the Bible but you're not always certain if you're reading His thoughts *out* of the text or your own thoughts *into* the text (you see the difference?), you need hermeneutics. If you belong to a Bible study group in which there are occasionally as many interpretations of a passage as there are participants around the table, you need hermeneutics.

Hermeneutics are the basic ground rules for interpreting the Bible. And all of the ground rules are founded on one important principle: *You must understand the context.* There are four kinds of context that we'll be considering in this section, the first of which is the Bible's historical setting. If we want to interpret the Bible correctly, we have to pay attention to the historical background of every passage we turn to. How do we do that? Let me spell it out in the form of three directives.

Pursue the Objective Facts

Some time ago, I read a book review of a new biography on the life of Ronald Reagan. According to the reviewer this biography contains a lot of fabricated information; the author has made up details about Ronald Reagan's life that are not completely true. However, the reviewer quickly added, the book tells a really good story and is well worth reading. I thought: *Huh? Who wants to read a biography that's not grounded on historical facts?*

Did you know that Christianity is unique among the world's religions in that it is grounded on historical facts? These facts are objective and verifiable. Take away the facts and the Christian faith crumbles. What *are* the facts? Well, according to the Bible's record, Jesus Christ, God's eternal Son, came to earth as a human being. He did miracles that provided evidence of His deity. Then He died on a cross to pay the penalty for our sins. And three days later He rose from the dead, proving that His sacrifice was effective and that He has the power to give people new and eternal life.

Take away these objective facts and there's not much left of the Christian faith. But that's not true of other world religions. Buddhism, for example, doesn't depend upon the historicity of its founder. It doesn't revolve around the life of *The Buddha*, Siddhartha Gautama, in 500 BC. It revolves around a set of teachings referred to as the Eightfold Path that will lead you to nirvana.

The same is true of Hinduism. Objective facts about Vishnu aren't important. Religious ideas are what hold Hinduism together. The same is true of Islam. Even though we know a lot about the actual life of Muhammad, Islam isn't built on the historical events of Muhammad's life. It's built on the Five Pillars of Faith as revealed in the Quran.

Christianity is the only major world religion that stakes its existence on objective facts. The apostle Paul drove home this point when he summarized the basic content of his teaching in the following verses:

Now, brothers, I want to remind you of the gospel I preached to you, which you received and on which you have taken your stand. By this gospel you are saved, if you hold firmly to the word I preached to you. Otherwise, you have believed in vain.

For what I received I passed on to you as of first importance: that Christ died for our sins according to the Scriptures, that he was buried, that he was raised on the third day according to the Scriptures, and that he appeared to Peter, and then to the Twelve. After that, he appeared to more than five hundred of the brothers at the same time, most of whom are still living, though some have fallen asleep. (1 Corinthians 15:1–6)

What does the apostle Paul say is the core of the Christian faith that he preaches? Christianity is grounded on certain objective facts: that Jesus died for our sins and was buried; that He rose again on the third day; and that scores of eyewitnesses actually saw all this! Take away those historical events and you lose the gospel, the good news of the faith. Take away those objective facts and "you [Christians] have believed in vain" (v. 2).

I heard about a very liberal theologian who was asked the question, "What if it could be proven beyond the shadow of a doubt that Jesus did *not* rise from the dead? What if Jesus' bones were discovered—verifiably—in a first-century tomb?" His reply: "That wouldn't make any difference to *my* faith. I would still believe that the spirit of Jesus is alive today."

What do you think about that theologian's response? I'll tell you what the apostle Paul would think about it. If we drop down to verse 14 of the passage we just read (1 Corinthians 15), Paul says: "And if Christ has not been raised, our preaching is useless and so is your faith." Genuine Christianity rests on objective facts.

Now, why am I making such a big deal about this point? What does this have to do with how we approach the task of understanding the Bible? Here's the reason for the big deal. The Bible's message is wrapped up in objective facts. If we want to interpret that message correctly, then we need to understand those objective facts. We need to understand the historical setting of whatever Bible passage we're looking at.

Are you following me? The Bible is *not* a Magic 8 Ball. Remember those? (Mattel, the toymaker, is still making them.) They were originally designed back in 1950 by a guy whose mother was a psychic. You ask the liquid-filled Magic 8 Ball a yes-or-no question, then you turn it upside down and an answer floats to the surface. The answer may be: *Outlook good;* or *Don't count on it;* or *Reply hazy, try again.*

Some people do this with the Bible. They open it to a random passage, hoping that it will speak directly to their lives, without any consideration of the historical facts behind that passage. If they open, for example, to the New Testament epistle of Colossians, they don't care *who* the Colossians were or *why* the apostle Paul was writing this letter to them. They just want a Magic 8 Ball message for *their* lives. If they open to the Old Testament book of Esther, they don't care *when* this story took place or *what* was going on in Esther's life at the time. They just want to know: What is this passage saying to *me*?

SOME PEOPLE open the Bible to a random passage, hoping it will speak directly. They just want a Magic 8 Ball message for *their* lives.

R.C. Sproul, a well-known theologian and author, tells an amusing story from his days of teaching at a Christian college.[1] One of his female students, a senior, found herself approaching graduation with no man in her life. Many of her friends had serious boyfriends or even fiancés.

So this young woman prayed for a guy. Then she got out her Bible and opened it at random to Zechariah 9:9: "Rejoice greatly, O Daughter of Zion! Shout, Daughter of Jerusalem! See, your king comes to you, gentle and riding on a donkey."

Now, if you know the objective facts behind this verse, you realize that it was written about 500 BC as a prophecy concerning a coming Savior; a prophecy that Jesus later fulfilled when He rode into Jerusalem on a donkey at the beginning of Holy Week. But this college senior interpreted Zechariah 9:9 as God's promise to provide her with a Prince Charming, even if he showed up on a donkey instead of on a white charger.

This is not good Bible interpretation (as I hope you already concluded). The historical setting of the passage we're reading matters. We must pursue the objective facts.

Cross the Cultural Rivers

One of my favorite *Far Side* cartoons shows a guy lecturing his dog. In the first of two panels, the guy says: "OK, Ginger! I've had it! You stay out of the garbage! Understand, Ginger? Stay out of the garbage or else!" The caption under this first panel reads: *What People Say*. The caption under the second panel reads: *What Dogs Hear*. What does Ginger hear? The thought bubble above her head says: "Blah, blah, blah, blah . . ." In case you missed the point of the joke, there's a formidable communication barrier between people and dogs.

There's even a formidable communication barrier between people when two groups of humans come from vastly different cultures. Have you ever experienced that? Have you ever tried to explain American football to a Brazilian friend, or been greeted with a bear hug by a Russian coworker whom you hardly knew? Or maybe you've been on one of your church's short-term mission trips to Haiti, Czech Republic, or Bangladesh. And you couldn't understand the language or the local customs.

One of my first mission trips, years ago, was to Amsterdam. Our Dutch hosts welcomed us with a meal. There was a milk bottle on the table that I assumed contained . . . well . . . milk. But as I poured it into my glass, it came out thick and lumpy. I just assumed that the milk wasn't homogenized and that the cream had floated to the top of the bottle. Well, I didn't want to pour it back, so I just drank it. Wow, was it sour!

Afterwards, one of the Dutch hosts asked me, "Is it the custom to *drink* yogurt in America?"

I quickly stammered, "Oh, yeah! Yogurt . . . of course. Love to drink that stuff."

As you read the Bible and *pursue the objective facts* that make up the historical setting of the passage you're looking at, you will also need to *cross some cultural rivers*. What I mean by that is: you will have to travel from *your* side of the river (a twenty-first-century, Western, technological society) to the *other* side of the river. If you're reading, let's say, the Old Testament book of Proverbs, the other side of the river is a tenth-century BC, Middle Eastern, agrarian society. If you're reading the New Testament epistle of 1 Corinthians, it's a first-century AD, Greco-Roman, urban society.

If you don't cross these cultural rivers, you won't understand much of what you read. For example, let's say that you're reading the Book of Ruth. Ruth is a destitute young widow. But she has a relative named Boaz who wants to help her out. Boaz wants to buy Ruth a piece of property, a place to live. Ruth 4:7 tells us that the guy who sells Boaz the property seals the contract by handing Boaz his sandal.

Now, that makes absolute sense to you, right? I mean, when you purchased *your* home and you went to the closing, didn't the seller hand you his shoe to seal the deal? He didn't? So, what's up with this sandal-passing business? In Ruth's day, this was the way for the seller to say: "The property that I used to walk on as my own now belongs to you." Pretty cool, eh?

We just crossed a cultural river. And we'll have to cross cultural rivers every time we pick up our Bibles, if we want to understand what we read, because we live in a time and place that's vastly different from Bible times and places. Now, you may be thinking, *But I could never do what you just did. That bit about handing over the sandal was amazing. How did you come up with that? Do they teach you that stuff at seminary? Was that from one of your doctoral courses?*

No, I think it was from a footnote in a study Bible. Most study Bibles have an introduction to every book of the Bible that explains the book's historical setting. A study Bible also has countless footnotes on every page that explain cultural phenomena. Think of a study Bible as a bridge that will enable you to cross cultural rivers. I recommend the *NIV Study Bible* for its wonderful explanatory footnotes. (The *ESV Study Bible* is a close runner-up.)

Ask the Journalistic Questions

I remember taking a class in journalism back in high school. And the teacher drilled into us that every good reporter relentlessly asks the five "w" questions: *Who? What? When? Where? Why?*

These are also good questions to ask whenever we read the Bible. Let me show you how this works. I'll ask each of the "w" questions for a couple of Bible passages. You'll quickly see how the answers to these questions help us interpret the passages.

Who Questions. We'll begin with the Ninevites. Here's a simple but key *who* question to ask: Who were these people that God asked the prophet Jonah to go and preach to? You probably remember certain aspects of this story. Take a look at the opening verses of Jonah:

> The word of the Lord came to Jonah son of Amittai: "Go to the great city of Nineveh and preach against it, because its wickedness has come up before me."
>
> But Jonah ran away from the Lord and headed for Tarshish. He went down to Joppa, where he found a ship

bound for that port. After paying the fare, he went aboard and sailed for Tarshish to flee from the Lord. (Jonah 1:1–3)

Now, it's never a good idea to try and run away from God. You can run, as the saying goes, but you can't hide. Jonah was eventually thrown overboard and ended up in the belly of a giant fish. That's when he decided that obeying God would probably be a good thing to do. So, the fish chucked him up and Jonah reluctantly fulfilled his mission. He preached to the Ninevites.

So, *who* were these guys? Why was Jonah so intent on staying miles away from them? If you don't know the answer to that question, you might assume that Jonah was just being rebellious. He rejected God's assignment because he thought he had better things to do with his time. Was that it? No. Jonah didn't want to go to Nineveh because he hated and feared its inhabitants. And we won't understand Jonah's hatred and fear toward them until we know *who* they were.

Unfortunately, the Bible passage we're looking at doesn't give us any details about the Ninevites. But here's the scoop—and it's information that I picked up from the *NIV Study Bible's* introduction to the book of Jonah. Nineveh was the capital city of ancient Assyria. Assyria was the superpower of Jonah's day and the Assyrians were notorious for the brutal way in which they treated the people they conquered. Some-

times they beheaded their victims and stacke
in piles. Other times they impaled their captiv
they skinned them alive.

So, if *you* were Jonah and
God sent you to the Ninevites,
wouldn't you jump on a ship in
the opposite direction? You can
see how knowing the *who* of a

**KNOWI.. ... .
of a Bible passage
enables us to better
interpret the text.**

Bible passage enables us to better interpret the text.

Let's try another *who* question. Who were the recipients
of 1 Corinthians 13, the apostle Paul's famous "love chapter"?
I'm sure you've come across the words of this text before.
They're often read at weddings. Or they're painted on wall
plaques. It's a nice, sweet passage on love. Probably written to
a nice, sweet group of people, right? Wrong!

The Corinthians may have been Christ followers, but
they were arrogant, divisive, gnarly Christ followers—which
is why the apostle Paul had to lecture them on the topic of
love. First Corinthians 13 is not meant to be nice and sweet.
It's meant to be in-your-face and tail-kicking. And now that
you know that little bit of historical background, open your
Bible and read verses 1–8 of that passage. I'm sure you'll see
the text with new eyes.

What Questions. Reading the Bible will raise all sorts of
what questions in your mind. For example, you're reading

Psalm 1 and you come to verse 4, where the psalmist describes those who don't meditate on and follow God's Word as *chaff*. Is that bad? Depends on the answer to the question: What is chaff?

Well, *chaff* is the thin, outer husk that surrounds a kernel of wheat. And in the ancient world, farmers would thresh their wheat by beating it up into the air—preferably on a day with a strong breeze. The hard kernels of wheat would fall to the ground and be gathered up. But the thin, outer husks, the useless *chaff*, would blow away. So, if you're not spending daily time in God's Word, the psalmist is warning you that you're wasting your life. Your life is just blowing away.

Here's another *what* question from a different passage: What is a firstborn? You say, "Now that's an easy one. A firstborn is the *first* one *born* into a family." Well, your definition creates a huge theological problem for Christians. You see, the apostle Paul refers to Jesus Christ as the *firstborn* over all creation (Colossians 1:15). According to your definition, Paul would be saying that God gave birth to Christ before He created everything else. But Christians believe that Christ is the *eternal* Son of God. He had no beginning. Maybe we'd better reconsider our definition of *firstborn*.

Let me tell you what's meant by this word. Sometimes the Bible uses *firstborn* to indicate a person's prominence. In the ancient world, a firstborn son was the heir to his father's fortune. He held a place of honor in the family. He had special rights and privileges. So the expression *firstborn* came to be used as a synonym for

SOMETIMES THE Bible uses *firstborn* to indicate a person's prominence.

most prominent one. That's why Psalm 89:27 refers to David as Israel's *firstborn* king. Now, we know that David wasn't the very first king of Israel. Saul was. But David was Israel's *greatest* king.

So when Colossians 1:15 calls Christ "the firstborn over all creation," it doesn't mean that He was the first created being, or that God gave birth to Him at some point in the past. It means that Christ reigns supreme over everything!

When Questions. Let's try a *when* question: When did the apostle Paul write the epistle of Philippians? Before I answer that question, let me tell you why it matters. The theme of Philippians is *joy.* Paul uses that word again and again and again in this New Testament letter. This is an amazing theme considering that Paul wrote Philippians *when* he was in jail! Not only that, he was in jail on trumped-up charges. I don't know about you, but I'm much more willing to listen to what a guy has to say about joy if he is joyful himself, even in the most adverse circumstances.

Here's another *when* question: When did Ruth live? In the most basic terms, that question is answered in the very first verse of the Old Testament book of Ruth. This is how Ruth 1:1 begins: "In the days when the judges ruled . . ." You say, "Big deal!" Well, let me tell you why it *was* a big deal. I referred to Ruth's story earlier in this chapter. She was the destitute young widow for whom

RUTH WAS a very godly, virtuous woman. But she didn't live in a godly, virtuous culture.

Boaz bought some property. Ruth was also a very godly, virtuous woman. But she didn't live in a godly, virtuous culture.

Ruth lived *in the days when the judges ruled.* The judges were the guys who led Israel before Israel had kings. And it was a dark era in Israel's history. In fact, the closing verse of the Old Testament book of Judges describes what that period was like with these words: "In those days Israel had no king; everyone did as he saw fit" (Judges 21:25). That's the world in which godly, virtuous Ruth lived. Have you ever complained about how hard it is to live a Christ-honoring life in a contemporary world that's irreverent, materialistic, violent, and sex-crazed? Meet Ruth—she can be a role model for you!

Just a footnote to this point about *when* questions. In *Epic*, the first book in the Bible Savvy series, I traced the storyline of the Bible from the beginning of creation (Genesis) to the eternal new heaven and new earth (Revelation). Once you learn that storyline you'll be able to place people and events in their appropriate historical settings as you come across them in your Bible reading.

When did Noah build his ark? *When* did Abraham and Sarah have a miracle son? *When* did Solomon rule over Israel? *When* did Ezekiel prophesy? *When* did Peter walk on water? *When* did Stephen get stoned to death? *When* did Timothy pastor a church? Can you place these events on a timeline? Did you know that I arranged the people just mentioned in chronological order? You would if you knew the Bible's storyline.

Where Questions. I'll just give you one *where* question: Where was Laodicea? The quick answer is that the city of Laodicea was located in a region which is part of modern-day Turkey. It was the site of a first-century church. This was one of seven churches to whom the apostle John penned letters, as recorded in Revelation 2 and 3.

John told the church at Laodicea that the risen and exalted Christ had a special message for them. The message was this (and I'll just paraphrase it for you): "Stop being spiritually lukewarm—or I'll spit you out of my mouth." That's not the sort of message that you want to hear from the risen and exalted Christ!

Here's the interesting thing about the language that Christ uses. Laodicea had a problem with its drinking water. The local river was muddy, so drinking water had to be brought in by an aqueduct. The water originated from a nice, cool spring five miles away, but by the time it traveled all the way to Laodicea it was tepid and unappetizing. One sip and you'd want to spit it out. So, because of *where* they lived, the Christians in Laodicea got Jesus' point when He warned them to stop being spiritually lukewarm.

The Bible raises a lot of *where* questions. It's extremely helpful to find out about places like the city of Jericho . . . the empire of Babylon . . . the Sea of Galilee . . . the church in Ephesus.

Why Questions. I could come up with a bazillion *why* questions to be asked as the Bible is read. But I'll give you just one example so you can understand what I'm talking about: Why did Elijah confront the false prophets of the pagan god, Baal, on Mt. Carmel? (You can read about this showdown in 1 Kings 18:16–40.)

Do you know this story? God's people had defected. Many of them had begun worshiping Baal. So God sent His prophet Elijah to duke it out with Baal's representatives. Elijah challenged them to a duel. These were his terms. Elijah said (my summary), "Meet me at the top of Mt. Carmel. I'll build an altar to my God. You build an altar to Baal. Then we'll both call upon our respective gods to send fire from heaven and consume the sacrifices on our altars. Whichever god answers is the one true God!"

Whoa! That was putting it all on the line. But *why* did

Elijah choose Mt. Carmel as the location for this heavyweight bout? Because Mt. Carmel was considered to be the dwelling place of Baal. In other words, Elijah was purposefully giving Baal home-field advantage. And that made the victory even bigger and better when Elijah's God was the only one who sent fire from heaven.

If we'll learn to ask *who, what, when, where,* and *why* questions as we read the Bible, we'll be amazed at how much more understandable and impactful God's Word becomes.

The overarching ground rule for interpreting the Bible is this: *You must understand the context.* In this chapter we covered the first of four kinds of context: the Bible's historical setting. How do we get a handle on this when reading Scripture? We *pursue the objective facts, cross the cultural rivers,* and *ask the journalistic questions.*

Sounds like work. Is it worth the effort? It is, if we want to hear God speak to us!

Study Guide
The Historical Setting

The *Study Guide* questions at the end of each chapter have been designed for your personal benefit. *All* questions can be used for personal study and, if you're part of a discussion group, for preparation for your group meeting. If you are part of a small group, you will find that the questions preceded by the group icon (👥) are especially useful for discussion. Your group leader can choose from among those questions when the group meets.

Icebreakers

Do you enjoy putting jigsaw puzzles together? Why or why not? Describe a key event or circumstance in your past that would provide others with some context for understanding who you are today.

1. What is hermeneutics? Why is it important for a proper understanding of the Bible? What is the most basic ground rule of Bible interpretation?

2. How does Christianity differ from most other major world religions when it comes to objective facts? What bearing does this have on how we interpret the Bible?

3. (icon) Have you ever traveled or lived in a foreign culture? If so, describe a few of the differences between that culture and your own.

   (icon) Why is it important to *cross the cultural rivers* when reading the Bible? (Or, what might happen if you don't cross the cultural rivers when reading the Bible?) What resource(s) will help you understand the culture of whatever Bible passage you're reading?

4. What are the five *journalistic questions* that should be asked of every Bible passage?

   For items 5–8, answer the expanded journalistic questions that are asked of each Bible text. Then you will have the opportunity to craft some journalistic questions of your own—and answer them—for a final passage.

5. (icon) Read Leviticus 16; then answer the following questions:

Who was Aaron (i.e., what unique role did he play in ancient Israel and what were the responsibilities of that role)?

What was the Most Holy Place—and *what* was so special about it?

When was Aaron allowed into the Most Holy Place? What is meant by the name given to this annual day?

Where was the live goat sent and what was the significance of that destination?

Why was the Day of Atonement to be a day of rest, when no work was done? (Hint: What does this say about the contribution that God expects from people in order for them to be forgiven?)

6. Read Joshua 3.

    Who was Joshua?

    What would be significant about crossing the Jordan River at flood-stage?

    When did this event take place in the history of ancient Israel?

    Where were Joshua and God's people headed?

    Why were the priests, who were carrying the ark of the covenant, the first ones to step into the water?

7. Read Luke 15:11–32.

    Who were the three major players in Jesus' parable—and *who* did each of them represent?

What was especially distasteful about the younger son's plunge to pig level? *What* was especially meaningful about the father's gift to this son upon the boy's return?

When did Jesus tell this parable (i.e., what occasioned it)?

Where did the father see the returning son—and what does that tell you about this dad?

Why was the older brother angry? *Why* had he been missing out on the blessings of his father's house?

8. Read 2 Corinthians 8:1–15.

   Who were the Macedonian believers and how did they differ from the Corinthians?

   What was Paul collecting money for?

When did Paul first raise the issue of giving toward this project with the Corinthians and what does that say about his bringing the subject up again in this letter?

Where did Paul draw the Corinthians' attention for an example of supreme generosity?

Why were the Corinthians not in a generous mood?

Now that you've gotten the hang of answering some journalistic questions, it's time for you to craft a few of your own. Create a who, what, when, where, and why question for the following passage. Then answer your questions.

9. Read Ruth 3.
   Who (somebody other than Ruth, since her profile has already been covered in this chapter) . . .

   What . . .

   When . . .

Where . . .

Why . . .

10. What did you learn from this exercise about the importance of understanding a Bible passage's *historical setting*?

{ 2 }
The Literary Setting

HOW WELL DO YOU know the field of sports? Here's a little sports trivia quiz: ten questions. Lock in your answers as you go. I'll give you the correct answers at the end of the quiz so that you can see how well you did.

In which sport would you:

1. Use a mashie or niblick?
2. Stand at a silly point?
3. Dial 8?
4. Throw stones at houses?
5. Do an eggbeater?
6. Employ the O'Brien shift?
7. Go 5 hole?
8. Use a box-and-one defense?
9. Make a nutmeg pass?
10. Be penalized for a crackback?

How did you do? You can match your answers with the following key and give yourself a grade. No cheating by changing your answers as you go. (None of this, "Oh yeah, that's what I really meant to say . . .")

1. *Golf.* The irons were called mashies and niblicks before Spalding Sporting Goods started naming them by number back in the 1930s.
2. *Cricket.* The fielding position closest to the batter is called a silly point. Maybe because you would be knocked silly if the batter hit you with his bat?
3. *Baseball.* Dial 8 is baseball slang for hitting a home run. Before 1970 that was the number you had to dial from a hotel phone in order to make a long distance call.
4. *Curling.* Don't ask me to explain throwing stones at houses (although I'm told the stone is the forty-two-pound disk you slide along the ice). I have serious reservations about even considering curling a sport.
5. *Water polo.* Because it's against the rules to go underwater in this sport (and drowning is strictly off-limits), players have to kick their legs in a circular motion like eggbeaters to stay afloat.
6. *Shot put.* O'Brien was a famous shot-putter and the first guy to face the back of the circle and do a 180-degree spin before releasing the shot.
7. *Ice hockey.* There are four corners of a net to aim at when you're shooting the puck. But the fifth target is

to go for the hole right between the goalie's legs.

8. *Basketball.* This is when four players set up a zone defense while the fifth player goes man-to-man (or woman-to-woman, as the case may be) with his opponent.

9. *Soccer.* Passing or dribbling the ball between the opposing player's legs is a nutmeg. The Australians call it a "nuttie." Enough said.

10. *Football.* This is an illegal block. One blocker more than two yards laterally from the incoming defensive player goes in motion and hits him below the waist. The defensive guy doesn't see the blocker coming and risks a major injury. You can understand why it's called a crackback!

Here's the point I want to make with this trivia quiz: All the answers come from the same world—the world of athletics. We're not talking about art or science or business or food here. We're talking about sports. However, even though all these activities are in the same category—sports—they're not at all alike. In fact, they're played by very different rules. If you sack the quarterback on a football field, for example, that's a good thing. But if you sack an opposing player on a basketball court, it's a technical foul. The same field of sports—but different rules.

The Literary Genre and
Rules of Interpretation

Well, that's how it is with the Bible. You may be used to looking at the Bible as a single volume, but it's actually made up of sixty-six books. And while all of those books belong to the same Bible, each one must be read according to its own rules of interpretation. In the last chapter you learned that the rules for interpreting the Bible are called *hermeneutics* and that the mother of all rules is: *You must understand the context*.

There are four contexts to be considered. The first is the historical setting of whatever Bible passage you happen to be reading. The second context, which is the focus of this chapter, is the literary setting. The books of the Bible represent a wide variety of literary genres. Genres is just a fancy word for *kinds*. As you read the Bible, you'll come across the following genres: laws, narratives (stories), poetry, proverbs, prophecies, epistles (letters), gospels (biographies), parables . . . and more. Some Bible books are just one genre; others may have two or more genres.

Each one of these literary genres must be interpreted according to its own rules. We're going to look at six of these genres and learn two or three rules for interpreting each of them. This is not a chapter to be read once and then set on a shelf. You'll want to keep a bookmark in these pages so that you can refer to them again and again, reminding yourself of the various rules that apply to whatever genre of biblical literature you're reading at the time.

How to Interpret Laws

There are over six hundred laws in the Bible, and all of them are found in books two through five of the Old Testament (Exodus through Deuteronomy). If you read *Epic*, you covered these books as you traced the Bible's storyline from beginning to end. You might remember that the biblical laws fall into three major categories.

There are *moral* laws that help God's people of every era determine right from wrong. There are *ceremonial* laws that enabled Old Testament believers to maintain a proper relationship with God. (Many of these laws had to do with priests, sacrifices, and the temple.) And, finally, there are *civil* laws that were used to govern the nation of Israel.

As you're reading through the opening books of the Old Testament and you come across one of these laws, the first rule for correctly interpreting it is this: *Determine whether the law is moral, ceremonial, or civil.*

Why is that important? Because only the moral laws are *directly* applicable to our lives today. (I'll say a word about laws that are *indirectly* applicable in a moment.) The moral laws are timeless. That's *not* the case with the other two kinds of laws. Ceremonial laws have been fulfilled by Jesus Christ, who is now our high priest, our sacrifice for sins, and the One who makes us into a temple for the Holy Spirit. And **ONLY THE moral laws *directly* apply to our lives today. The moral laws are timeless.** civil laws, strictly speaking, were for regulating community life in ancient Israel.

Let's practice distinguishing between different kinds of laws by sampling a chapter from the book of Leviticus. You may want to turn in your Bible to Leviticus 19, since we'll be looking at a variety of laws in this chapter. First, let's look at verse 18: "Do not seek revenge or bear a grudge against one of your people, but love your neighbor as yourself. I am the Lord."

OK, which kind of law is this: moral, ceremonial, or civil? It's obviously a moral law, which means it's still in force today. It prohibits revenge-seeking and grudge-holding. Are you mad at somebody? Are you determined to give them the same bad treatment they've given you? God's law says, "Stop it! Ask God to help you love that person."

But now look at the very next verse: "Keep my decrees. Do not mate different kinds of animals. Do not plant your field with two kinds of seed. Do not wear clothing woven of two kinds of material" (v. 19).

What do you think? Which kind of law are these? Do

they sound like moral laws to you? No, they're actually ceremonial laws. Let me explain why. When we traced the Bible's storyline in *Epic*, through the *Books of the Law*, I pointed out that God chose the nation of Israel for a special purpose. They were to be a blessing to all other nations by lighting the way to the one true God. This was their mission. They were set apart for this unique purpose.

Do you recall how God helped them remember that they were set apart and different from everybody else? God gave them ceremonial laws like the ones you just read in Leviticus 19:19. Laws that commanded them to separate different kinds of animals or seeds or fabrics (i.e., just as God had separated them from other people). These laws are not for us today. It's OK to plant carrots alongside tomatoes in your vegetable garden. It's OK to wear the blouse that blends cotton and rayon. (Just make sure it goes with the rest of your outfit. You don't want to break any *fashion* laws!)

So, *the first rule for interpreting an Old Testament law is to determine whether the law is moral, ceremonial, or civil.* And, by the way, this rule will come in handy when defending God's Word against various social critics today. Gay activists, for example, will often argue: "Sure, there's an Old Testament law that prohibits homosexuality. But there's also a law that prohibits cooking a young goat in its mother's milk. C'mon! Neither one of these laws makes any sense in today's culture."

That argument stems from bad hermeneutics. It misinterprets the Bible. The Old Testament law that prohibits homosexuality is a moral law, which means it's timeless. Still applicable today. But the law that prohibits cooking a young goat in its mother's milk is ceremonial. It describes a common idolatrous ritual that was practiced by the nations surrounding Israel, which is why God commanded His Old Testament people to steer clear of it. But this is hardly a practice we have to worry about today.

Now, let me throw in one disclaimer with regard to this first rule for interpreting an Old Testament law: It won't always be obvious whether a law is moral, ceremonial, or civil. (Sorry.) We've been sampling laws from Leviticus 19. Here's one more from that chapter: "Do not cut your bodies for the dead or put tattoo marks on yourselves. I am the Lord" (v. 28).

I get asked about tattoos all the time. Does this verse apply to us today or not? Either way, it's not my intention to make you uncomfortable if you already have a tattoo. Chances are, you didn't even know about this verse before you got the tat. So, what are we to make of this Old Testament law?

Bible scholars hold two very different interpretations of this prohibition against tattoos. Some say that the tattoos in Leviticus 19:28 were part of a pagan grieving ritual in Old Testament times. That would make this a ceremonial law, prohibiting participation in this ancient pagan ritual. So it would no longer be applicable. But other Bible experts say that this law fits with a broader biblical theme: we have been made in the image of God and so we shouldn't deliberately do anything that mars our body. That would make this a moral law. It's still valid today.

Which is it: moral or ceremonial? Well, if you already have—or would like to get—a tattoo, you'll probably nonchalantly dismiss this law as ceremonial. But if you favor caution, you might want to interpret this as a moral law and stay out of tattoo parlors. (How's that for dodging the issue and remaining friends with all my readers?)

Here's *the second rule for interpreting the Bible's laws: Look for the principle behind the law.* Most moral laws are pretty straightforward. The principle is obvious. It's clear what God wants you to do—or *not* do. But sometimes the principle is buried beneath the cultural trappings of Bible times and you'll have to dig it out in order to apply it to contemporary life. Let's take another look at Leviticus 19: "When you reap the harvest of your land, do not reap to the very edges of your field or gather the gleanings of your harvest. Do not go over your vineyard a second time or pick up the grapes that have fallen. Leave them for the poor and the alien. I am the Lord your God" (vv. 9–10).

How do you apply these laws to your life if you're not a Bible-times farmer or vineyard owner? Well, you *look for the principle behind the law.* What's the principle here? God commands us to provide food for the poor. That's something every one of us can do today by dropping off canned goods at the local food pantry, or by contributing to our church's special offering for disaster relief, or by some other means.

Now, let me point out something interesting about these laws regarding food for the poor that we've just looked at. They're actually *civil* laws. They had to do with the governing of society in ancient Israel. They comprised ancient Israel's welfare system. But didn't I previously make the point that we don't have to obey the Old Testament's civil laws? Didn't I say that they're not for us today? Only the moral laws are applicable, right? Generally speaking, that's correct. But here's an interesting insight. When we discover the principle behind a law, even the civil and ceremonial laws become *indirectly* applicable to our lives.

WHEN WE discover the principle behind a law, even the civil and ceremonial laws become *indirectly* applicable to our lives.

I've just given you an example of what the principle behind a *civil* law looks like (i.e., provide food for the poor). Let me do the same thing with a *ceremonial* law. The book of Leviticus has several chapters of laws that deal with the treatment of infectious skin diseases. When you read these laws for the first time, you're liable to think, *This is gross stuff. What is it doing in the Bible? And what significance could these laws possibly have for me?*

Well, these were ceremonial laws, part of Israel's religious life. So, on the one hand, we could dismiss them as no longer applicable today. But on the other hand, there's a principle behind these laws that *is* applicable to our lives. At a deeper level, the skin disease laws are a reminder to stay away from sinful behaviors that would compromise a readiness to be used by God. God wants His people to be set apart from sin so that they're primed to carry out their special mission.

Keep that principle in mind the next time you read about skin rashes or leprosy in Leviticus. Say to yourself: "God wants me to deal with sin in my life as seriously as I'd deal with a gross or deadly disease. Then I'll be spiritually prepared to point others to Him." Get it?

So, for good biblical interpretation (hermeneutics), remember and practice the two rules for interpreting Old Testament laws: (1) Determine whether the law is moral, civil, or ceremonial; and (2) look for the principle behind the law.

How to Interpret Narratives

Narratives are stories. Over one-third of the Bible comes to us in this form. All of the Old Testament's *Books of History* (from Joshua to Esther) are collections of narratives. So are the New Testament's Gospels and book of Acts. I wonder if God teaches us through narratives because He knows that nobody can resist a good story. Young and old, educated and uneducated, Easterners and Westerners—we all love stories.

The Bible is full of engaging stories: Israel crossing the Red Sea on *terra firma*; Samson falling for a hairdresser by the name of Delilah; David taking down the giant Goliath with a slingshot; Jonah being swallowed—and later chucked up—by a giant fish; Jesus multiplying a boy's brown-bag lunch to feed thousands; Peter being sprung from jail by an angel. And none of these Bible's stories is made up. They're all true. They describe a supernatural God intervening in the lives of ordinary people.

Let me give you two rules for interpreting narratives. First, *summarize the theme (or major lesson) of the story.* Unfortunately, the Bible doesn't do this for us. At least, not explicitly. The narratives don't conclude with the words: "And so, the moral of this story is . . ." Have you ever read a story that ends like that?

I'll tell you a quick one. It's about a guy named Benny. (No, this isn't in the Bible, so don't start flipping through the pages to find it there.)

Benny was out exploring ancient ruins one day and he came across a Grecian urn. When he wiped off the urn with his handkerchief, a genie appeared. But this wasn't a nice genie offering Benny three wishes. This was a genie who was ticked off at having been disturbed. So, she put a curse on Benny. (I can't believe I'm telling you this story.) She said, "You must never shave, for on the day that you shave I'll turn *you* into an urn." So Benny never put a razor to his face.

But eventually Benny's beard got so long and straggly and itchy that he just had to shave it off. The minute he finished the job the genie appeared and—*poof*—she turned Benny into an urn. And so, the moral of this story is (can you guess?): *A Benny shaved is a Benny urned!*

OK, OK. That was pretty lame. But I want to illustrate the fact that—contrary to how Benny's story concluded—the Bible's stories rarely come right out at the end and tell us the moral, the theme, the major lesson of the story. It's our job to figure it out. And the reason that it's a good idea to try figuring it out is that this exercise keeps us from misinterpreting the *details* of the story. I've heard some pretty whacked-out interpretations that people have pulled out of Bible narratives because they've read way too much into a minor detail or two.

What is the theme of the *whole* story? Why do you think God included this story in His Book? And here's something else to keep in mind while you're

THE REAL HERO of every narrative in Scripture is *God*. Reflect on what *God* is up to in the Bible story.

trying to sum up the theme of a story. Remember that the real hero of every narrative in Scripture is *God*. So reflect on what *God* is up to in the Bible stories you read.

For example, Genesis 39 relates the story of Joseph and Mrs. Potiphar. Mrs. Potiphar was the wife of Joseph's boss and she had the hots for Joey. She tried to seduce him. One day she grabbed Joey by his coat and said: "Come to bed with me!" (I'm not making any of this up. It's all in Genesis 39, as well as in the popular musical *Joseph and the Amazing Technicolor Dreamcoat*. Go, Donny Osmond!) Do you know what Joseph did? He left his coat in Mrs. Potiphar's hand and ran out of the house.

An obvious theme (major lesson) that we could take away from this story is that we should flee (i.e., run away as far and fast as possible) from sexual temptations. That works. But there's a bigger theme behind *that* theme. Joseph wasn't the only hero in the story. What about *God*? If you go back and read Genesis 39 in context, you'll discover that God was watching over Joseph's life every step of the way because He had big plans for the young man. Joseph eventually became Pharaoh's second-in-command and was given the job of overseeing a famine-relief program. Among those he was able to feed were his very own brothers, thus keeping his family alive. And hundreds of years later that family line produced a descendant named *Jesus*!

That's the really big theme behind the Joseph and Mrs. Potiphar story. If God had not rescued Joseph from this lady's sexual advances, Jesus' ancestors would have starved to death. There would have been no family line stretching to Jesus. I've heard a friend of mine, who's a brilliant Bible scholar, put it this way: "*God* enabled Joseph to keep his pants zipped up so that *God* could later give the world a Savior." A bit crudely put? Perhaps. But you won't forget *that* theme.

Here's a second rule for interpreting narratives: *Decide what's descriptive and what's prescriptive.* Some details of Bible stories are merely *descriptive.* They give us the particulars of what happened. They are not meant to be a pattern for our lives. But other details of Bible stories are *prescriptive.* God is indeed saying to us readers today, "This is how I want you to respond in similar situations."

How can we tell the difference between what is *descriptive* and what is *prescriptive*? Very simply, the *prescriptive* parts of a story will always be backed up by non-narrative, directive passages in other parts of the Bible. Let me illustrate what I'm talking about with a couple of Bible stories. I'll go back to the Joseph and Mrs. Potiphar story for my first example. Was Joseph's running away from sexual temptation *descriptive* or *prescriptive*? In other words, are we being told something that's just part of *that* particular story (*descriptive*) or is God saying to us: "I want you to do the same thing that Joseph did when you're faced with sexual temptation" (*prescriptive*)?

I think Joseph's behavior is *prescriptive*. Why do I say that? Because there are a number of non-narrative, directive passages in the Bible where we're told to run away from sexual temptation. Proverbs 5:8 cautions guys to keep their distance from tempting women. The apostle Paul warns Timothy to "flee the evil desires of youth" (2 Timothy 2:22). So Joseph's 100-yard dash in the opposite direction of sexual allurement is *prescriptive* for all of us.

JOSEPH'S 100-yard dash from sexual allurement is *prescriptive* for all of us.

Let's try another story—the story of the Holy Spirit's outpouring on first-century believers (Acts 2). This event takes place fifty days after Jesus' resurrection and return to heaven. The disciples are waiting in Jerusalem for the Holy Spirit, whom Jesus had promised to send them. Suddenly, the Spirit shows up and fills them and they begin to speak in different languages (literally, *other tongues*). Is this experience of tongues *descriptive* or *prescriptive*?

Some Christ followers (usually my charismatic or Pentecostal brothers and sisters) say: "It's prescriptive. We should all speak in tongues, once we've put our trust in Jesus and He's filled us with the Holy Spirit." But wait a minute! The Acts 2 account also says that flames of fire appeared over the heads of those that the Holy Spirit filled. Should we also expect flames of fire over *our* heads? (I don't know too many people who believe *that*!)

No, I think that this is a *descriptive* passage. This is what happened to Jesus' original followers. But it's not *prescriptive.* There are no non-narrative Scripture passages telling us that we *must* speak in tongues as a sign of the Holy Spirit's filling. That doesn't mean that I don't believe in the filling of the Spirit or the *gift* of tongues. I do! The apostle Paul talks about this gift at length in 1 Corinthians 12 and 14. Some Christ followers obviously have it. But the gift of tongues is never spoken of in the Bible as a *must* for every believer today.

So two rules prevail for interpreting narratives: 1. Summarize the theme (or major lesson) of the story. 2. Decide what's descriptive and what's prescriptive.

How to Interpret Poetry

I owe my marriage to poetry. When I was a junior in college, I wrote Sue a proposal poem and set it to music. Then I sang it to her, accompanied by my guitar, under a shady tree on campus.

Between the second and third verse of the song, I pulled out a ring box and handed it to Sue. By the time I was done with verse three and the chorus, she was mine. She didn't stand a chance against my poetry. Poetry is powerful stuff!

Poetry makes up over one-third of the Bible. There are entire Bible books that come to us in this form: Job, Psalms, Proverbs, Song of Songs, and Lamentations. Many of the *Books of Prophecy* are also filled with poetry.

Here are three quick rules for interpreting Bible poetry. I mostly have in mind here the poetry in the book of Psalms. In fact, if your Bible is still within reach, you may want to turn to Psalm 51. We'll be applying rule one to the opening verses of this psalm:

> Have mercy on me, O God,
> according to your unfailing love;
> according to your great compassion
> blot out my transgressions.
> Wash away all my iniquity
> and cleanse me from my sin.
>
> For I know my transgressions,
> and my sin is always before me. (vv. 1–3)

Rule number one is to *note the historical background.* Do you know the historical background of this poem of confession? (In the case of this psalm, the header before verse 1 gives it away.) King David had an affair. He got his neighbor Bathsheba pregnant. And Bathsheba's husband was one of David's most loyal soldiers, a guy named Uriah. Do you recall how David dealt with his sin? Initially, he tried to cover it up. He instructed one of his generals to abandon Uriah in battle. After Uriah was killed, David married the widow, which made it appear as if Bathsheba's pregnancy was on the up and up.

All his tracks covered, right? Not from God's eyes. God sent a prophet, Nathan, to deal with David. It was a pretty intense toe-to-toe confrontation. (You can read about it in 2 Samuel 12:1–13.) But David finally broke and Psalm 51 is his prayer of confession. This poem marks the beginning of a long road back. Just knowing the historical background to Psalm 51 increases your understanding of the poem immeasurably, doesn't it?

There's a historical background to be discovered for many of the psalms. There's also a *historical background* to Song of Songs (King Solomon's love poem), the poetic messages of the prophets, and to most of the poetry you'll find in the Bible. Check it out.

Here's a second rule for interpreting Bible poetry: *Unpack the figurative language.* The language of poetry is colorful and highly emotional. Many of the words and expressions are meant to be understood *figuratively*, not *literally.* The poet is painting word pictures.

Let's go back to David's confession of sin in Psalm 51. Look at verse 7: "Cleanse me with hyssop, and I will be clean; wash me, and I will be whiter than snow." What does David

65

mean by that phrase, *cleanse me with hyssop*? Here's the scoop: hyssop is a tall reedy plant, with a head of bushy leaves. It looks like a giant paintbrush. And that's one of the most notable ways it was used in Bible times.

Do you remember the story of Israel's deliverance from slavery in Egypt? Pharaoh needed some convincing to let God's people go. So, God sent an angel of death to slay all the firstborn humans and animals in Egypt. But God's people were spared, having identified their homes by covering the doorframes with the blood of a sacrificed goat or sheep. The angel of death passed over these places (which is why this event has been celebrated ever since as *Passover*). What role did hyssop play in this story?

HYSSOP BECAME associated with God's mercy—the turning aside of God's judgment.

Hyssop was the giant paintbrush that God's people used to spread the blood on their doorframes. As a result, hyssop became associated with God's mercy—the turning aside of God's judgment.

Now do you see the tremendous significance behind David's prayer? "Cleanse me with hyssop, and I will be clean." David was pleading with God for forgiveness based upon the shed blood of sacrifices. We voice a similar prayer today when we ask God to forgive us because of Christ's death on the cross. If we've put our trust in Jesus Christ, His blood has been applied to our lives, causing God's judgment to pass over us. (Interestingly, the only mention of hyssop in the New Testament is when a sponge full of wine vinegar was extended to Jesus as He hung upon the cross.)

You'll find a lot of *figurative* language in the Psalms whose meaning will have to be unpacked. In the familiar Psalm 23, as another example, David describes God as his shepherd and himself as a sheep that longs to "lie down in green pastures" and be led "beside quiet waters" (v. 2). Doesn't that sound refreshing to you? Sounds good to me! In Psalm 116, David cries out: "The cords of death entangled me" (v. 3). That, too, is poetic language. David wasn't *literally* tied up with ropes. He just felt like his troubles were wrapped around him and pulling him into a dark pit. Ever felt that way?

We all express ourselves, from time to time, with *figurative language*. When you exclaim, "I could strangle that guy who cut me off in traffic," I hope you're not *literally* contemplating murder. When you say, "I bombed that chemistry test," I'm guessing you didn't bring explosives to school. Bible poetry uses colorful, highly emotional *figurative* language. Sometimes it's dark. Sometimes it's rich and inspiring. Savor it. Meditate on what it's saying.

One final rule for interpreting Bible poetry: *Look for truths about God*. This is especially applicable when you're reading Psalms. In the Bible as a whole, we find over 250 names and titles and attributes that describe God. The book of Psalms is a gold mine for those descriptors. You can't read a single psalm without learning a ton about God.

BIBLE POETRY uses highly emotional figurative language. Sometimes it's dark. Sometimes it's rich and inspiring.

So, try reading the psalms out loud and stopping every time you come across one of God's names, titles, or attributes. Take a moment to praise God for what that particular word or expression tells you about Him. In fact, you could do this with every bit of poetry that you come across in Scripture— even the passages where the prophets are denouncing other nations for their brutality against Israel. Note what those poems teach you about *God*, then praise and worship Him along those lines.

So here are the three rules for interpreting Bible poetry: 1. Note the historical background. 2. Unpack the figurative language. 3. Look for truths about God.

How to Interpret the Proverbs

When you're reading the Old Testament book of Proverbs, there is just one key rule to follow: *Remember that proverbs are not absolute promises but statements about how life usually works.* Why don't you turn in your Bible to the book of Proverbs and we'll take a look at several examples of what I'm talking about.

> Honor the Lord with your wealth,
> with the firstfruits of all your crops;
> then your barns will be filled to overflowing,
> and your vats will brim over with new wine.
> (Proverbs 3:9–10)

This proverb encourages us to tithe—to give God the *firstfruits* (the first 10 percent) of our income. If we'll do this, God will see to it that we prosper. Is this an *absolute promise*? Is tithing a sure way to grow rich? Will people who give to the Lord never lose their jobs? No. But, generally speaking (*generally speaking* is the operative phrase), tithers will experience God's blessing on their lives in a variety of ways (e.g., answers to prayer, intimacy with God, freedom from worry.).

Now consider this verse from Proverbs 15:1: "A gentle answer turns away wrath, but a harsh word stirs up anger." If we put this proverb into practice, will 100 percent of the people who argue with us calm down? No. Some of them will still lose it. But, generally speaking, a gentle answer is a good way for us to resolve a conflict.

Here's the advice of Proverbs 22:6: "Train a child in the

way he should go, and when he is old he will not turn from it."
So if we raise our kids in a godly home environment, they'll
never rebel, right? Well, I've known some great parents whose
kids wandered far from God and some of those kids never
came back. If this proverb is an *absolute promise*, then those
parents must have somehow messed up in their child-raising.
Because if they hadn't messed up, their kids would still be
walking with God. No! This is not an absolute promise. It's
a statement of how life usually works. If we'll invest time and
effort in the spiritual training of our children, moms and dads,
most often it will pay off in their lives.

Next, let's look at two verses from Proverbs 26 that, at
first glance, may seem to contradict each other. Beginning
with verse 4, we're told how to answer a fool: "Do not answer
a fool according to his folly, or you will be like him yourself."
If we interpreted this verse as an *absolute*, we would never
ever respond to someone who's acting like a jerk toward us.
We would always just ignore him, refusing to stoop to his
level.

However, look at the very next verse of Proverbs 26: "Answer a fool according to his folly, or he will be wise in his own
eyes" (v. 5).

What is this verse saying? Evidently, it's sometimes wise
to *ignore* a fool (v. 4) and it's sometimes wise to *correct* a fool
(v. 5). If either of these proverbs were applied in an *absolute*

manner, it would cancel out the other one. No. They are both examples of *how life usually works* and the reader should apply whichever one seems most appropriate in a given situation.

One footnote to this rule for interpreting proverbs: Always keep in mind that the power for putting the proverbs into practice has to come from God. These are not just *self*-help principles. Proverbs isn't like a *self*-improvement book that you order through Amazon.com. You can't do it by yourself. A relationship with God is required if you want to benefit from the Bible's proverbs. The Holy Spirit must be living in your life.

Years ago, my dad taught a Bible study for businessmen in Chicago's Loop. He used Proverbs as his curriculum because there's a lot of good counsel regarding wise business practices in this Old Testament book. Some of the guys who attended his Bible study weren't Christ followers. They were just attracted to the group by the helpful content of the study. So, it was important for my dad to regularly remind them: "You won't really benefit from this stuff until you put your trust in Christ and begin a relationship with God. Then God's Spirit will empower you to live wisely."

Here's the single rule for interpreting proverbs: Remember that proverbs are not absolute promises but statements about how life usually works.

Interpreting Prophecy

As I pointed out when tracing the Bible's storyline in *Epic*, there are more Bible books that fall into the *prophecy* category than any other. Sixteen of the Old Testament books are prophetic, written by four major prophets (so called because they wrote *longer* books) and twelve minor prophets (so called because they wrote *shorter* books). Only one book of the New Testament, Revelation, is predominantly prophetic. But there are scores of prophetic passages in other New Testament books as well.

Please remember that much of what you read in the Old Testament *Books of Prophecy* has very little to do with predicting the future. The vast majority of what the prophets have written simply confronts sin in people's lives and urges them (and us) to turn back to God. The confronting sin portions of Bible prophecy are fairly straightforward, so I won't take any time to explain how to interpret those passages.

But let me give you a couple of rules for interpreting prophecies that have to do with predicting the future. First, *distinguish between what has already been fulfilled and what—as yet—is unfulfilled.* Let's suppose that an Old Testament prophet told God's people in 750 BC about something that would happen in the future. And let's suppose that what he predicted actually came true 150 years later. Question: Would the fulfillment of that prediction be in *our* future? (This is not a trick question.)

No. The fulfillment of that prediction would be history for us. It would have come true in 600 BC (if we've done the math correctly). Are you following this? Why is this an important point? Because we often assume—wrongly—that Old Testament prophecies about future events have to do with events in *our* future. We're looking *ahead* to see their fulfillment. But we should look *behind* because many of these predictive prophecies have to do with events that have already taken place.

This means that it's important to know our Bible history. Knowing Bible history will enable you—when you're reading in Isaiah or Daniel or Amos—to distinguish between what has already been fulfilled and what—as yet—is unfulfilled. Where do you go to learn about Bible history? By now you probably know my standard answer to that question. Pick up *a study Bible* (I recommend the NIV) and read the Old Testament *Books of Prophecy* with the aid of all those helpful historical introductions and footnotes.

KNOW BIBLE history to distinguish between what has been fulfilled and what—as yet—is unfulfilled.

Here's a second rule for interpreting prophecy: *Distinguish between figurative descriptions and literal descriptions.* This rule is especially important to keep in mind when you're reading the New Testament book of Revelation.

Will the Antichrist—that despotic ruler who takes over the world in the end times—*literally* have ten crowned horns on seven heads, as described in Revelation 13:1? I don't think so. As I explained when I covered the Revelation portion of the Bible's storyline in *Epic*, this is a *figurative* description of a leader who will have a vast amount of political and military power.

Will the capital city of the eternal new earth *literally* measure 12,000 stadia long (roughly 1,400 miles) by 12,000 stadia wide by 12,000 stadia high, as described in Revelation 21:16? I doubt it. I think that's a *figurative* description of a city, which is cube-shaped because a cube represents the presence of a triune God (Father, Son, and Spirit).

Bible prophecy teachers, who speak on Christian radio stations and write bestselling books, are frequently guilty of providing us with way too many *literal* details that they've drawn out of very *figurative* prophetic passages. Be careful of these experts! Most often they don't even agree with each other in their interpretations.

Again, distinguish between figurative descriptions and literal descriptions. Granted, sometimes you won't be able to resolve whether a description is figurative or literal. Let me give you the biggest example of this dilemma in the Bible. There are many Old Testament prophetic passages that talk about a future day when God will restore the nation of Israel to a place of prominence in the world. Now, there are two *huge* schools of interpretation with regard to these prophecies.

One school says that they're to be taken quite literally. In fact, the re-creation of Israel as a nation-state in 1948 may be the beginning of the fulfillment of these prophecies, so say the Bible scholars who belong to the *literal* school.

But another school of Bible scholars interprets these prophecies about Israel figuratively. Its members point out that the New Testament speaks of Christ followers as "the Israel of God" (Galatians 6:16), heirs of the promises that were made to Abraham (Galatians 3:14, 29). So all the Old Testament prophecies that have to do with Israel's future should now be applied to the church, the corporate body of Christ followers.

This *figurative* school of interpretation teaches, for example, that chapters 40 through 48 of Ezekiel, describing a future temple in Jerusalem, are not about an actual building that's eventually going to replace the current Dome of the Rock. Ezekiel was describing a group of people who would become a temple for the Holy Spirit. Who would that be? Us! Followers of Jesus Christ.

I'm not going to resolve the debate between these two schools in this book. I'm just trying to make you aware of the challenge and the need to distinguish between figurative descriptions and literal descriptions when interpreting Bible prophecy. So hold your conclusions humbly and loosely.

What are the two rules for interpreting prophecy? First, distinguish between what has already been fulfilled and what—as yet—is unfulfilled. Second, distinguish between figurative descriptions and literal descriptions.

Interpreting the Epistles

There are twenty-one epistles in the New Testament, thirteen of them written by the apostle Paul. Many readers find these letters to be among the easiest portions of the Bible to interpret and apply because their teaching is so direct and because they're written to fellow Christ followers (not citizens of ancient Israel). We'll still need a few rules, however, to ensure accuracy when interpreting epistles.

The first rule is a drum that I keep beating and beating: *Discover the historical background*. This applies to whatever epistle you're reading. (And should I say *consult your study Bible* one more time?) Bible scholars sometimes refer to the New Testament epistles as *occasional* letters because the writing of each of them was *occasioned* by certain circumstances. It helps if you know those circumstances. Otherwise, it will be difficult to interpret the epistles.

Imagine this: You take a letter out of your mailbox and,

without looking at the front of the envelope, you tear it open and begin to read it. Unfortunately, the mailman has delivered the letter to the wrong house. It belongs to your neighbor. It's been written by a friend of his, who immediately launches into a lengthy discussion of circumstances that you know nothing about.

What are your chances of accurately interpreting that letter? (Not that you *should* be interpreting the letter, since you're reading your neighbor's private correspondence. Put it back in the envelope.)

Here's an example from a New Testament epistle that will illustrate the importance of *discovering the historical background* of whatever passage you're reading. Let's say that you pick up the apostle Paul's first letter to the Corinthians and you begin reading at chapter seven. In the opening verse of this chapter, Paul writes: "It is good for a man not to marry" (1 Corinthians 7:1).

So Paul is down on marriage, eh? He must be a big fan of celibacy. Whoa! Not so fast! This is the same Paul who wrote to the Ephesians that marriage is a model of Christ's relationship with His followers (i.e., the church). That doesn't sound like someone who wants to discourage people from getting married, does it?

Seems like a real disconnect, right? Well, knowing the historical background to Paul's first letter to the Corinthians helps make sense of what's happening. The letter's recipients were falling prey to all sorts of sexual immorality. People in the church were even rationalizing liaisons with prostitutes. One church member was having an affair with his stepmother—and nobody seemed to think it was a big deal.

In that sort of an environment, it was appropriate for Paul to raise a yellow flag for those who were considering marriage. The Corinthians needed some basic teaching on God's standards for sexual expression before they sent out any wedding invitations. That's why Paul wrote to them, "It is good for a man not to marry."

The second rule for interpreting the epistles: *Read the epistle in its entirety before trying to interpret parts of it.* Isn't that how we usually read a letter that somebody has sent to us?

When I was a college student, I fell in love with Sue. And shortly thereafter I took a job in Europe for the summer. We'd write each other several times a week, four to five pages at a shot. (No such thing as international cell phones or Skype back then! This was just a few years after the Pony Express quit operating.)

Whenever I got a letter from Sue that summer, I would immediately stick it in the back pocket of my jeans, and pull it out in fifteen-minute intervals to read it. The first time I pulled it out, I would randomly read the fifth paragraph on the third page. Then I'd put the letter back in my pocket.

Later, I'd pull it out again and choose the second paragraph on the first page. Put the letter away. Pull it out later and read the seventh paragraph on the fifth page.

Are you buying my story? Of course not! Nobody reads a letter like that. The first time through you read it from beginning to end. Now, you may go back later many times to a favorite paragraph or two—but only after you've read that letter in its entirety.

That's how to read a New Testament epistle: *not* in bits and pieces (at least, not initially) but *in its entirety.* Then you can go back and take it apart, a paragraph or a chapter at a time.

Here's the third rule in interpreting a portion of a Bible epistle: *Summarize the main point of the passage.* I've already mentioned this rule for other types of Bible literature, so I won't elaborate on it here. Let me note again, however, that the reason people often misinterpret the Bible is because they tend to pull out minor details and then blow them out of proportion. The easiest way to avoid making this mistake is to evaluate each passage you read as a whole.

READ A NEW Testament epistle not in bits and pieces (at least, not initially) but *in its entirety*.

You've probably heard the saying: *I can't see the forest for the trees.* This can happen to you when you're reading the

Bible. You can stand with your nose so close to the individual trees that you miss the overall forest. Step back from specific verses and *summarize the main point of the* (entire) *passage.*

Once more, the three rules for interpreting epistles are: 1. Discover the historical background. 2. Read the epistle in its entirety before trying to interpret its parts. 3. Summarize the main point of the passage.

Put It All Together

Are you ever going to remember all the rules that were spelled out in this chapter? Not right away. But if you'll put a bookmark in these pages, pull out the rules each time you begin reading a new book of the Bible, and review the two or three rules that apply to that book's *literary* setting, over time you will gain a greater and greater understanding of God's Word.

It's kind of like taking golf lessons. The instructor adjusts your stance, messes with your grip, reminds you to keep your head down, shows you how to address the ball, explains the importance of a smooth backswing, warns you to follow through, follow through, follow through. And then he says: "OK, let's see you put it all together."

Seems impossible!! And all those instructions are just for your tee shot. What about your irons in the fairway? (Your mashie and your niblick?) What about your chip shots to the green? What about your putting?

You'll catch on—if you'll just stick with it. And once you catch on, golfing will be a joy (well, sometimes). Let me tell you, there's no greater joy than learning to skillfully interpret God's Holy Word so that the Bible begins to transform your life.

To watch Jim's midpoint comments about Context, scan this QR code with your smartphone or go to www.biblesavvy.com/video/#context2.

Study Guide
The Literary Setting

Icebreaker

What genre of literature do you enjoy the most—and why?

1. Although baseball, football, and basketball all come from the world of sports, they are played by very different rules. What does this analogy teach us about interpreting the Bible?

2. Why is it bad hermeneutics to dismiss the Old Testament law that prohibits homosexuality on the basis that some other laws are obviously obsolete?

3. Read the fourth commandment in Exodus 20:8–10. This is a difficult law to categorize because it seems to qualify as two different kinds of law. Which two? (Pick from *moral*, *ceremonial*, and *civil*.) Explain your answer. (Romans 4:5 may help you identify one of the categories.)

What principle(s) do you see behind this law (i.e., how is it applicable today)?

4. Read the brief story in Matthew 8:5–13. What is the overall theme of this narrative? Which elements of the story seem to be *descriptive* and which ones are *prescriptive*?

5. Many of David's psalms praise God for delivering him from his enemies. What are some of the probable backstories to these psalms of deliverance? (If you're unfamiliar with the Old Testament, take a look at 1 Samuel 17:32–50, 1 Samuel 18:6–11, and 2 Samuel 15:1–14.)

How does knowing the backstories to David's psalms of deliverance help you apply these psalms to your own life?

6. Isaiah 55:1–3 is an example of the poetry that can be found in the *Books of Prophecy.* Explain the figurative language in these verses. (What are the *wine, milk,* and *bread* that Isaiah is referring to?) How does Isaiah's poetry here make his message more poignant?

(•••) What do you learn about God from this brief snippet of poetry?

7. What's the single rule for understanding proverbs? What danger will you run into if you fail to heed this rule?

(•••) How would this rule impact your understanding of Proverbs 16:3's application to your life?

8. Why is it important to know Bible *history* when interpreting prophecies about *future* events?

9. 〖☺☺☺〗 What are the two different ways to read all the prophetic passages about the future restoration of the nation of Israel?

10. Find out the occasions (purposes) that prompted Paul to write the following epistles. You will need a study Bible to locate this information

Romans

1 Corinthians

Galatians

Philippians

1 Thessalonians

Philemon

11. How might you retain the rules you learned in this chapter for future use as you read the Bible?

{ 3 }
The Theological Setting

YEARS AGO, SUE AND I were visiting my parents in the town where I grew up. I'd heard about a new church in town, so on Sunday I suggested to Sue that we check it out. It was only about a mile from my parents' home and a balmy summer day, so we decided to walk. When we got there we discovered that the church was meeting in a converted warehouse—which we thought was pretty cool!

There were only thirty to forty people in attendance, mostly young like us, and everybody seemed to know each other. The worship band was decent, kicking off the first part of the service.

And then the pastor got up to preach. His text was from Exodus 28. Before I ask *you* to read it, let me give you some background to the passage. God has just instructed His people, as they're traveling from Egypt to the Promised Land, on how to build a large tentlike tabernacle for the purpose of worship. Now God turns to the subject of designing priestly garments for Aaron. Aaron was Moses' brother and the guy who was going to officiate at the tabernacle.

Here's the text:

Make the robe of the ephod entirely of blue cloth, with an opening for the head in its center. There shall be a woven edge like a collar around this opening, so that it will not tear. Make pomegranates of blue, purple and scarlet yarn around the hem of the robe, with gold bells between them. The gold bells and the pomegranates are to alternate around the hem of the robe. Aaron must wear it when he ministers. The sound of the bells will be heard when he enters the Holy Place before the Lord and when he comes out, so that he will not die. (Exodus 28:31–35)

When the pastor finished reading this text, I wondered: *Where's he going to go with this? And how could he possibly draw any meaning from this passage for our lives?* I didn't have to wonder for long. The pastor immediately zeroed in on the gold bells and the pomegranates that adorned the hem of Aaron's robe. (Buckle up. You're about to go for a ride.) Beginning with the pomegranates, he made the observation that these are a type of fruit. (Uh-huh.) And elsewhere in the Bible, he pointed out, the apostle Paul talks about godly character as the *fruit* of God's Spirit, which consists of "love, joy, peace, patience, kindness, goodness, faithfulness, gentleness and self-control" (Galatians 5:22–23).

The pastor said that our lives should be marked by this sort of fruit. I thought to myself: *I understand what Galatians 5:22–23 says about the fruit of the Spirit—but I'm still not sure what that has to do with the pomegranates on Aaron's robe in Exodus 28.* But the pastor wasn't finished. He turned from the pomegranates to the golden bells. He said that the golden bells represented the *gifts* of the Spirit "because bells are something that we give each other as gifts." This was news to me. I'd never given anybody a bell as a gift in my entire life.

By now the pastor had picked up a head of steam, and he was really getting into his sermon. He said that of all the gifts or special abilities that God's Spirit gives us, the most important one is tongues—that supernatural enablement to speak in an unknown language. The pastor spent the better part of the next hour (yes, *hour*) telling us why this gift was a *must* for every Christ follower. And then he closed by asking us to bow our heads in prayer. While our heads were bowed, he invited us to lift a hand in the air if we wanted to signal a desire for the gift of tongues.

He repeated the invitation again and again . . . and again. The band began to play softly. I was quietly hoping that some poor soul would lift his hand, so the pastor would wrap things up. And that's when it dawned on me: *We're the only outsiders in this group. He's waiting for Sue and me to lift our hands.* I suddenly felt like there was a huge bull's-eye painted on my chest. At that point, I leaned over to Sue and whispered: "We're outta here!" And with that, we slinked out of our seats, burst out the back door of the place, and didn't stop running for about three blocks—because we were sure they were gonna come after us!

Question: What's to keep people from reading whatever they want into the Bible? What's to keep them from making the Bible say whatever they want it to say (even about pomegranates and bells)? There must be some rules to follow in order to interpret the Bible correctly. There are! These rules are called hermeneutics, and they're founded on the major premise: *You must understand the context.*

WHAT'S to keep people from reading whatever they want into the Bible?

There are four kinds of context to consider when reading a passage from the Bible. So far, we have considered two of those contexts—the Bible's *historical* and *literary* settings. We are now ready to take a look, thirdly, at the Bible's *theological* setting. Now, don't let the word *theological* scare you off. Theology has to do with the study of various themes that we find in Scripture. I will cover three aspects of what it means to consider the Bible's theological context in the following pages.

The Principle (and Its Application)

There's a very important principle to consider when looking at a Bible passage from a theological perspective. Here it is: *The Bible must always agree with itself because it all comes from the same Mind.* Whose mind is that? *God's* mind! Take a look at a couple of key Scripture verses that back up this truth (they are well worth memorizing):

All Scripture is God-breathed and is useful for teaching, rebuking, correcting and training in righteousness. (2 Timothy 3:16)

For prophecy never had its origin in the will of man, but men spoke from God as they were carried along by the Holy Spirit. (2 Peter 1:21)

These two verses focus on the fact that *God* is the ultimate author of the Bible. There may have been many human authors responsible for the writing itself—but they were writing down exactly what *God* wanted to say.

Now, this is an important point to make, because in the last two chapters we've focused on the *human* authors of Scripture, not the *divine* author. And that focus has tended to highlight the Bible's diversity. That diversity is seen, first of all, in the unique historical setting (recall chapter 1) of each human author. As I point out in *Foundation* (the second book in the Bible Savvy series), forty different human authors contributed to the Bible, writing at different times over a 1,500-year period, on three different continents, in three different languages. That's diversity! And when these human authors put pen to parchment, they expressed themselves through diverse literary settings (chapter 2), including laws, narratives, poetry, and prophecy.

But now as we come to the Bible's theological setting, we move from an emphasis on *diversity* to an emphasis on *unity*—because we move from a focus on the Bible's *many* human authors to a focus on the Bible's *one*, ultimate Author: God. This is the basis of the principle for interpreting the Bible with theological accuracy: *The Bible must agree with itself because it all comes from the same Mind.*

Maybe an analogy would be instructive here. I love to read mysteries. And my favorite kind of mystery writer is one who lays out several threads of storyline before beginning to weave them together. So, in the first chapter of the book, we're introduced to a few characters and the circumstances of their lives. But as we begin to read chapter two, there may be no mention of these original characters. Instead, we may be introduced to some entirely new people and some entirely new circumstances. It's almost as if we're beginning to read an entirely new book.

However, we're certain that as we continue to read, all

these different characters and their different circumstances are going to fit together, right? How can we be so sure of that? Because we know that the same author is behind the entire story. So, if we read something in one part of the book that seems to conflict with something in another part of the book, we can rest assured that it will all jibe . . . eventually. The apparent conflict will disappear.

What does this have to do with interpreting the Bible? Recall the main principle behind our consideration of the Bible's theological setting: *The Bible must always agree with itself because it all comes from the same Mind.* God is not going to disagree with Himself! What He says in one portion of His Word will not be out of sync with what He says in other portions.

That's why the best way to check if your interpretation of a Bible passage is correct is to compare that interpretation with what the rest of the Bible teaches on the same subject. Are there supporting passages that back up what you think you're seeing in a particular text?

This leads to the critical application of the theological principle that I've been driving home: *The best tool for interpreting the Bible is the Bible.* If the Bible must always agree with itself (the principle), then we should constantly be comparing our understanding of specific texts with what the Bible teaches elsewhere (the application).

This, by the way, is why the leaders of the church's

Reformation in the sixteenth century put such an emphasis on getting people into the Bible. At the time, the popular notion was that only those in the church's hierarchy (priests and theologians) could accurately interpret God's Word. So people were discouraged from trying to read the Bible on their own. If they did, it was argued, they were bound to misunderstand it. "Baloney!" objected the Reformers. (Only they said "Baloney!" in Latin). Their objection was captured in a rallying cry: "*Sola Scriptura*!" ("The Bible alone!"), which is just another way of saying: The Bible itself can keep readers from misinterpreting the Bible.

THE BIBLE itself can keep readers from misinterpreting the Bible.

It's the best tool we have for understanding God's Word.

Now, before I move on to some examples of how to use the Bible to interpret the Bible, let me add a note of clarification to the basic principle that *the Bible must always agree with itself because it all comes from the same Mind*. Sometimes that agreement is not apparent. And that's frequently due to what theologians refer to as *progressive revelation*.

What do Bible scholars mean by *progressive revelation*? Well, there are many things that God reveals to us in Scripture *over time*. In other words, the earlier writings in the Bible may introduce a concept to us that isn't further developed until later writings. So, if we compare this concept in the Bible's earlier writings with the same concept in the later writings, it may seem as if the Bible *disagrees* with itself. But it's not disagreement—it's development. It's *progressive revelation*.

Let me give you a couple of quick illustrations of *progressive revelation*. The first illustration has to do with the Bible's major storyline. If you read *Epic*, you hopefully can recall the single word that sums up that storyline: *redemption*. From the beginning of time, people have gotten themselves into trouble with a Holy God because of their sin. Fortunately, God has a plan for redeeming us from the penalty and the power of our sin. And that plan revolves around a Savior.

Now, when that Savior is first introduced to us in the third chapter of the Bible, the introduction is very cryptic. All that we're told is that one day a descendant of Adam and Eve (i.e., a human being) will crush Satan—but in the process of doing so, he will be severely wounded (Genesis 3:15). That's a foreshadowing of Jesus Christ and His death upon the cross, but we don't get all that information in Genesis.

However, if we keep reading the Bible, we learn some additional things about the coming Savior. We learn that He's going to come from the line of Abraham, the people of Israel, and yet He will be a blessing to the entire world (Genesis 12). Later we learn that He will eventually be a great king like David, whose reign will last forever and ever (2 Samuel 7). Still later we learn this Savior will die a violent death—but in doing so, He will pay the penalty for people's sins (Isaiah 53).

And then we come to the New Testament. The opening four books—the Gospels—describe the actual arrival of this Savior. His name is Jesus Christ. He does miracles. He dies on a cross. He rises from the dead. Amazing events—but their full significance is not explained in the Gospels. It's not until we get to the New Testament epistles that Paul and a few other apostles tease out what was accomplished by the life, death, and resurrection of Jesus—and how it applies to our lives. And it's not until the very last book of the New Testament, Revelation, that we get a riveting picture of Christ's future reign over an eternal kingdom.

What's the point of my brief Bible survey here? To demonstrate that God sometimes reveals things to us in His Word a little bit at a time. This is *progressive revelation.* So, when you're using the Bible to interpret the Bible—keep that in

GOD SOMETIMES reveals things to us in His Word a little bit at a time.

mind. Don't assume that one part of the Bible is at odds with another part of the Bible, when it may just be a case of God gradually unfolding some truth to us.

Let me give you another, far less grand illustration of *progressive revelation.* It has to do with monogamy: one man married to one woman. This is God's design for every marriage, right? Well, Kody Brown doesn't think so. Kody has his own TV reality show called *Sister Wives*. He's a fundamentalist Mormon who is married to four women.[1] But when I say *fundamentalist Mormon*, don't think of a guy in bib overalls, living in a cabin in northern Utah. Kody is a forty-one-year-old ad salesman, sporting feathered hair and a goatee, who drives a Lexus two-seater sports car.[2] And his latest wife is fairly good looking. (Not that I noticed.)

Where does Kody get the bizarre notion that it's OK with God to be married to four women at one time? He probably thinks he gets it from the Bible. So let me quickly review what the Bible has to say about monogamy. For starters, it seems this is God's original plan for marriage, since Genesis 2:24 says that "a man will leave his father and mother and be united to his wife, and they will become one flesh." That's *one* man and *one* woman becoming *one* flesh—a not-too-subtle endorsement of monogamy.

However, it wasn't long after Adam and Eve fell from grace that men started taking multiple wives. And some of these polygamous husbands were heroes of the faith: Abraham; Jacob; David; Solomon. Surprisingly, nowhere does Scripture condemn their behavior! I'm sure that Kody is taking his cues from guys like these. So, should we let go of our insistence on one-wife-per-husband? NO! Consider God's *progressive revelation* on this score.

To begin with, even though the Bible describes some of the heroes of the faith as taking multiple wives, it also describes this pattern as always leading to trouble. Solomon's many wives even turned his heart against God! (See 1 Kings 11:3–4.) Next, when Jesus arrives on the scene, He reiterates what Genesis 2:24 says about a husband and wife becoming *one* flesh. And then He adds this line (Matthew 19:6): "So they are no longer two, but one." Did you catch that? Jesus did *not* say, "So they are no longer three, but one" (or "five, but one," as in the case of Kody Brown).

And the Bible has still more to say about monogamy. By the time we get to the epistles of the apostle Paul, we read that monogamy is a mark of spiritual maturity (1 Timothy 3:2). Please keep in mind that Paul wrote that to people who were living in a polygamous culture. So the biblical standard for marriage is one man joined inseparably to one woman.

The complete picture of God's plan comes into total focus through progressive revelation. While we use the Bible to interpret the Bible, we must always make sure that we've read God's *latest* word on any subject.

The Examples

OK, let's take a look at three examples of how we can use the Bible to interpret the Bible, as we consider the topics of prayer, hell, and baptism.

Prayer. Our first test case has to do with prayer. In Luke 11, Jesus' disciples observe Him praying one day. They're so impressed by what they see that they ask Jesus to teach *them* how to pray.[3] In the middle of Jesus' ensuing tutorial on prayer, He says, "Ask and it will be given to you; seek and you will find; knock and the door will be opened to you. For everyone who asks receives; he who seeks finds; and to him who knocks, the door will be opened" (Luke 11:9–10).

Now, what if this were the only passage in the Bible that we had on prayer? Jesus promises, "Ask and it will be given to you." And He repeats His promise in the next verse, "Everyone who asks receives." So I fold my hands, close my eyes, lift my voice to God, and pray, "Lord, please give me a million dollars!" Does that work? It hasn't worked for me.

You may object, "Well, you can't ask God for something like a million dollars. It has to be something legit." But where does Luke 11 say *that*?

Luke 11 *doesn't* say that. However, there is more than one passage in the Bible on prayer, and 1 John 5:14–15 *does* say that! First John 5:14–15 reads: "If we ask anything according to [God's] will, he hears us. And if we know that he hears us—whatever we ask—we know that we have what we asked of him." So, it's not simply a case of "ask and it will be given to you"—like we read in Luke 11. No, what we ask God for has to be *in accord with His will*, as we learn in First John 5.

You see what I just did? I used the Bible to interpret the Bible. But we're not yet finished with this topic of prayer. Let's say that I pray and ask God for something that's *in accord with His will*. Let's say, for example, that I'm out of work and pray for a job. I think it's reasonable to assume that God would want me to be employed. So, based on Luke 11, combined with 1 John 5, I pray for a job, and next week I'm hired, right?

Not so fast! Let me tell you a few more things that the Bible says about getting answers to prayer. Luke 18:1 says that sometimes I've got to keep on praying and not give up. Evidently, the answers aren't always right around the corner. So God may want me to pray for a month for that job . . . or a year. Mark 11:24 says that I've got to pray with faith. I've got to believe that I've already received from God what I've prayed for. What else does the Bible teach about getting answers to prayer?

James 4:1–3 says that I must be free of selfish motivations when I pray. If I want that job strictly so that I have money to spend on me and my family—and if I don't have a track record of giving a portion of my income to the Lord's work— my prayer may fall on deaf ears. And, finally, John 15:7 says that my prayers are most effective when I am personally maintaining a close relationship with Christ. "If you remain in me," says Jesus, "and my words remain in you, ask whatever you wish, and it will be given you." Do I desire to spend time in God's Word (i.e., allowing Jesus' words to remain in me) as much as I desire the new job I'm praying for?

We've just constructed a *theology* of prayer. Instead of misinterpreting what one verse in Luke 11 teaches about prayer ("ask and it will be given to you"), we've sur-

INSTEAD OF misinterpreting what one verse teaches about prayer, survey other passages in the Bible to get the full scoop.

veyed other passages in the Bible on the topic as well. Now, we've got the full scoop. We've used the Bible to help us interpret the Bible.

Hell. Here's another example of how this works. The topic is hell. It's a topic that occasionally makes it into the secular news. Not too long ago a very popular megachurch pastor wrote a book on the subject that became headline material. I watched him launch this book on the Internet, as he was interviewed by the religion editor of *Newsweek* magazine in New York City. It was said that more viewers were watching this interview than any previous Internet event of a similar kind.

According to the book's author, God *loves* people so much that He's going to see to it that nobody winds up in hell—unless they really, really want to go there. Love will carry the day. God's love will triumph over human resistance.

(The book's title, *Love Wins*, underscores this notion.) The author told his interviewer that he was not just making this stuff up. This is what the *Bible* teaches. I'm sure he had in mind verses like John 3:16: "God so loved the world that he gave his one and only Son." God *loves* the world. And John 3:16 concludes by saying that the aim of God's love is to see to it that people "shall not perish but have eternal life." So, it is obvious that God wants people to have eternal life and not spend eternity in hell.

However, is that *all* the Bible teaches on the topic of hell? *God loves people*—is that it? Interestingly, if we drop down just two verses below John 3:16, this is what John 3:18 says: "Whoever believes in him [Jesus Christ] is not condemned, but whoever does not believe stands condemned already because he has not believed in the name of God's one and only Son." Those who don't believe in God's Son—Jesus—stand condemned. What happened to God's *love*?

We need to keep in mind that love is not God's only attribute. God is also holy, righteous, and just—which means that He must punish wrongdoing; He must punish sin. The only way to avoid that punishment is to

LOVE IS NOT God's only attribute. God is also holy, righteous, and just—which means that He must punish wrongdoing.

put our faith in the Savior that God has provided. Jesus is that Savior, because Jesus took the punishment we deserve when He died on the cross. That's why those who reject Jesus stand condemned before God. They're hell-bound.

And speaking of Jesus—nobody in the Bible talked more about hell than Jesus. Jesus frequently warned His listeners not to end up there. He told them to fear the one who has the power to "destroy both soul and body in hell" (Matthew 10:28). That's a strange teaching if this contemporary author's dismissive view of hell is true.

We can't pull out isolated Bible verses on a topic. We've got to consider what the *whole* Bible says about the matter. That's the *theological* context.

Baptism. One final example of how this works. Let's look at a Scripture passage about baptism. In Acts 2, the apostle Peter preaches the first Christian sermon on record. This is just a month and a half after Jesus' resurrection from the dead and His return to heaven. Peter is on the streets of Jerusalem, a huge crowd is in town for a religious holiday, and Peter is preaching like there's no tomorrow. Look at these closing words of Peter's sermon.

"Therefore let all Israel be assured of this: God has made this Jesus, whom you crucified, both Lord and Christ." When the people heard this, they were cut to the heart and said to Peter and the other apostles, "Brothers, what shall we do?" Peter replied, "Repent and be baptized, every one of you, in the name of Jesus Christ for the forgiveness of your sins. And you will receive the gift of the Holy Spirit." (Acts 2:36–38)

Aren't you a little surprised by what Peter tells the crowd to do in order to be forgiven by God, "Repent and be baptized"? The *repent* part makes sense to us—that just means to turn away from our sins and turn toward Christ. That's a faith decision. And the Bible tells us that we're saved by faith. But what about the *be baptized* part of Peter's response? Is Peter adding some sort of religious ritual, some sort of good deed to the salvation equation? Must people be baptized in order to have their sins forgiven? (Some Protestant denominations teach this, based upon verses like Acts 2:38.)

Let me review what other Bibles verses teach on how we are saved:

For it is by grace you have been saved, through faith— and this not from yourselves, it is the gift of God—not by works, so that no one can boast. (Ephesians 2:8–9)

He saved us, not because of righteous things we had done, but because of his mercy. (Titus 3:5)

However, to the man who does not work but trusts God who justifies the wicked, his faith is credited as righteousness. (Romans 4:5)

Verses like these make it clear that God saves us on the basis of our faith in Christ—not because we've been baptized (or on the basis of any other good work). Then how are we to understand Peter's emphasis on baptism in Acts 2:38? We must conclude that Peter is *not* saying that baptism is a requirement for forgiveness. That would be out of sync with what the rest of the Bible teaches. On the other hand, Peter *is* saying that people who genuinely put their faith in Christ for forgiveness will be eager to publicly affirm that decision by getting baptized. Baptism ought to be a slam dunk (sorry) for *true* Christ followers.

The Tools

As you were tracking with my three examples (*prayer, hell, baptism*) of how to use the Bible to interpret the Bible, perhaps you were thinking to yourself: *This is easy for Jim to do with his theological training. But I could never do this.* Oh, yes you could! It just takes the right tools.

It's amazing how much easier a job becomes when we have the right tool for it. Years ago, I decided to save some money by changing the oil in my car by myself. I'm not very mechanically inclined, but fortunately there's not a whole lot to this process. It's just a case of draining out the old oil, replacing the filter, and putting in a few quarts of fresh oil. Simple! Except for the fact that my filter was screwed on very tightly and wouldn't budge. Besides that, it was in an awkward place to reach and extremely difficult to get a grip on with my oily hands. I must have tried for an hour to get that sucker off before giving up and going to the auto supply store for some advice. Their advice was to buy one of their oil filter wrenches. Which I did, and took it home. I had my filter off in twenty seconds!

When it comes to correctly interpreting the Bible *theologically*, it helps to have the right tools for the job. The apostle Paul told his friend Timothy that he should approach the Bible like a skilled workman "who correctly handles the word of truth" (2 Timothy 2:15). In the same way that a carpenter knows how to use his miter box and a surgeon knows how to wield her scalpel and a baseball player knows how to swing his bat, Christ followers should know how to use the tools that make them expert Bible handlers.

Here are four tools that will help you understand the Bible's *theological setting* of any significant topic that you come across in your reading.

Cross-references. Your Bible probably has a column that runs down the middle (or perhaps the margin) of every page.

That's the list of cross-references. When you're reading a verse that raises an interpretive question in your mind, look to see if there is a tiny letter of the alphabet above any of the words or phrases in that verse. That letter corresponds to one or more

FOUR TOOLS will help us understand the Bible's theological setting on any significant topic: cross-references, a concordance, a study Bible, and a systematic theology.

cross-references listed in the middle column (or margin).

For example, we looked at Luke 11:9 while discussing prayer. The second phrase of that verse says, "Ask and it will be given to you." Now, in my Bible, there's a tiny *j* above that phrase. So, I go to the middle column of the page. I look for verse 9 of chapter 11. I find the tiny *j*. And it gives me one cross-reference. A cross-reference is a verse in another part of the Bible that says something about the same topic.

Great! Next to the tiny *j* it says: Matthew 7:7. So I look up Matthew 7:7. Now, unfortunately, this is not initially very helpful, because Matthew 7:7 says the exact same thing, with the very same words, as Luke 11:9. So this was a waste of my time, right? Nope. Hang in there with me. There's a tiny *q* in the middle of Matthew 7:7. So I go to the tiny *q* in the middle column of cross-references, and you know what I find? No less than 11 other Bible passages that deal with the topic of how to ask God for stuff in prayer. By looking up these other verses and noting what they teach about prayer, I am kept from misinterpreting Luke 11:9's promise: "Ask and it will be given to you."

A concordance. Most Bibles have a concordance at the back. (They're located just before the maps that most of us never look at.) A concordance is an A–Z list of the most common words that appear in the Bible. After each word, you'll find a bunch of Bible verses that use that word. So if you want to know what else the Bible has to say about prayer, after reading Luke 11:9 you can turn to the *p*'s in the concordance and look up *prayer, pray, praying.* There are a lot of verses on that topic.

Or, if you want more information on *hell*, you can look up *hell* under the *h*'s in your concordance. However, let me mention an interesting side note with regard to this particular topic. When I looked up *hell* in my Bible's concordance, I discovered that all the references are in the New Testament. Should that bother me? Is the contemporary author, whom I referred to earlier, correct when he says that we make too big a deal out of hell (i.e., since it isn't even mentioned in the Old Testament)? No. Instead, this is another instance of *progressive revelation.* The fact is the Old Testament has little to say about the afterlife—hell or heaven. That's a matter that God reveals in greater detail in later books of the Bible.

A study Bible. This is a wonderful tool for interpreting God's Word. The footnotes and book introductions in a study Bible typically include theological insights. For example, if you'll go to the passage in Acts 2 where Peter tells his audience that they need to *repent and be baptized* in order to be forgiven, you'll find a footnote (in the *NIV Study Bible*) that offers the very explanation that I gave you a moment ago for how baptism fits with a salvation that is received by faith alone.

I've found the *NIV Study Bible* to be so helpful that I purchased a second copy of it for my iPhone. It was worth the $25 to have this electronic tool at my fingertips whenever I want it.

A systematic theology. This is a textbook that covers almost any Bible topic you could think of. You just look up the topic in the index at the back of the book and it will direct you to the pages where the author discusses that topic. There are many systematic theology textbooks from which to choose. My favorite is written by Wayne Grudem and entitled, appropriately, *Systematic Theology* (Zondervan), and I recommend it frequently to others (all of our church's staff members and elders have a copy) for several reasons.

First, Dr. Grudem is a highly respected theologian and Bible scholar. Second, he is fair and gracious when presenting differing positions on controversial issues. Third, he knows how to put the cookies on the bottom shelf for the average reader. His book is very understandable—even enjoyable and devotional.

Keep in mind, too, that this is not a volume you must sit down and read cover to cover; it is over 1,200 pages. It's more like a reference tool that you'll keep on your bookshelf and turn to when you have a theological question about something you've read in Scripture. In fact, I encourage the leaders of our 300-plus small groups to keep a copy of Grudem's *Systematic Theology* on their shelf, so that they can find answers to the tough questions that pop up in any good Bible study.

Don't Know Much About Theology?

An old love song occasionally resurfaces in a retro version, called "Don't Know Much about History." The singer confesses that while he doesn't know much about history, biology, geography, or other school subjects, he *does* know that he loves his girl. Cute. Most of us smile when we hear those lyrics, because we identify with a guy who feels limited in his knowledge of academic subjects. Such ignorance is usually not a big deal (unless you're a doctor who's singing "don't know much about biology"). It's much more important to be in love.

Unfortunately, many Christ followers have a similar attitude toward theology. They view it as an academic subject that they don't know much about—but, hey, they love God. And that's all that matters, right? Not quite. The problem with such a cavalier dismissal of theology is that it fails to recognize the fact that we theologize every time we pick up a Bible and read it. We come to conclusions about what each passage says about God, or about various other topics. Those conclusions may be accurate or they may be seriously flawed. In other words, we may have good theology or bad theology—but we all come away from the Bible with a theological perspective on what we've read. Theology is unavoidable. So it's imperative that our theology be accurate.

Hopefully, this chapter has challenged and equipped you to become a skilled workman (or workwoman), who "correctly handles the word of truth."

Study Guide
The Theological Setting

Icebreaker

Does the word *theology* have a positive or negative ring in your ears? Explain.

1. Why must the Bible, given its wide diversity of human authors, always agree with itself? What is the practical application of this principle? Explain why this is so.

2. How does progressive revelation account for the fact that sometimes the Bible seems to disagree with itself?

3. Write out a theology of prayer based upon the Scriptures and insights covered in this chapter.

4. Using the concordance in your Bible, summarize what Jesus teaches about hell.

5. 🗨️ Read John 3:1–21. Choose three words that you find interesting and that are cross-referenced in your Bible. Write down what you learn about each of these three words from looking up the cross-references.

First word:

Second word:

Third word:

6. 🗨️ Read Colossians 2. Now, read it a second time, along with all the corresponding footnotes in a study Bible of your choice. Record the top three insights that you gleaned from these footnotes. (Remember that you can purchase an *NIV Study Bible* app for your iPhone and begin using it in the next five minutes!)

7. 🗨️ Jesus says in Mark 10:11 that "anyone who divorces his wife and marries another woman commits adultery." Period! If this were the only biblical text on divorce, you would have to conclude that divorce is always prohibited—no exceptions. But using your Bible's concordance, cross-references,

and footnotes, construct a fuller theology of divorce (i.e., especially noting if there are any circumstances in which God permits it).

8. In what sense is every Bible reader a theologian? Why should this motivate you to pay attention to theology as you're reading the Bible?

{ 4 }
The Immediate Setting

A FRIEND RECENTLY SENT me a humorous article he'd found on the Internet entitled: "Reasons Why the English Language Is Hard to Learn."[1] Here are some of the compiler's observations about the strange way in which we use words:

> There is no egg in eggplant nor ham in hamburger.
>
> Why is it that writers write but fingers don't fing, grocers don't groce, and hammers don't ham?
>
> Doesn't it seem crazy that you can make amends but not one amend?
>
> If a vegetarian eats vegetables, what does a humanitarian eat?
>
> In what language do people recite at a play and play at a recital?
>
> How can a slim chance and a fat chance be the same, while a wise man and a wise guy are opposites?

You have to marvel at the unique lunacy of a language in which your house can burn up as it burns down, in which you fill in a form by filling it out, and in which an alarm goes off by going on.

The writer makes a sharp point: Words, in any language, can be difficult to interpret. And for Bible readers that creates problems, because the Bible is made up of words. In order to avoid misunderstanding what these words are meant to communicate, we must follow some basic ground rules of interpretation: *hermeneutics*.

Do you recall the foundational principle behind hermeneutics? *You must understand the context*. And so far we have considered three important contexts that will help us accurately interpret God's Word. The first of these has to do with the *historical* background of any passage we read. Where did the events take place? What was happening at the time?

The second context worth noting is the *literary* setting of each passage. Is it a narrative, or a poem, or an epistle? There are different rules for interpreting each literary genre.

Third, there are *theological* issues raised in every biblical text. We must be careful not to read too much into what one passage says about a topic without comparing our interpretation with what other Bible passages say about the same topic.

We are now ready to take a look at a fourth, and final, interpretive context. This is the *immediate setting* in which we find the words that we read in Scripture. Words cannot be understood in isolation. Only when they are used in a sentence does their meaning becomes apparent.

Let me illustrate what I'm talking about with the word

spring. (I owe this illustration to Duvall and Hays' excellent book on hermeneutics, *Grasping God's Word.*[2]) This English word may refer to one of four things: a season; a metal coil; an act of jumping; or a source of water. It's impossible to answer the question, "What does *spring* mean?" with any precision until it is used in a sentence.

If I say, "I hope we don't run into a dry *spring* ahead," two of the four possible definitions are eliminated right away. It's obvious that I'm not talking about a metal coil or an act of jumping. However, there are still two definitions remaining. I could be referring to the approach of a season that's lacking in rainfall, or I could be leading a caravan through the desert to a worthless watering hole. Which dry *spring* is it? Let me add one additional sentence to the immediate context of my original statement: "I hope we don't run into a dry *spring* ahead. The grass and flowers need lots of rain before the heat of summer. " Aha! Now you know that the *spring* I have in mind is a season of the year.

What determined the meaning of this word? Its *immediate setting*—the way it was used in a sentence, followed by the way that sentence was used in conjunction with a second sentence. In this chapter we will explore how a word's setting in a particular Bible passage helps us interpret that word accurately.

Many Bible words—some very important ones—can be

just as difficult to pin down as the English word *spring*. Take, for example, the Greek word *sarx*. A very succinct and literal translation of this word is *flesh*. What does *sarx/flesh* mean? The New Testament uses this word in a variety of ways.

In Romans 3:20, the apostle Paul writes that "no one [*sarx*] will be declared righteous in his [God's] sight by observing the law." Paul is obviously referring to humanity in general by his use of *sarx* in this verse. But that's clearly *not* what he means by *sarx* when he tells the Corinthians that "there was given me a thorn in my flesh" (*sarx*, 2 Corinthians 12:7). This is a reference, no doubt, to Paul's body. Jesus also used *sarx* to refer to His body—but not to His body as a whole. He spoke specifically of the non-skeletal parts of it: "a ghost does not have flesh [sarx] and bones, as you see I have" (Luke 24:39). And then there is the spiritual use of *sarx* that Paul regularly employs to speak of our sinful nature: "Those controlled by the sinful nature [sarx] cannot please God" (Romans 8:8).

One word, multiple meanings. Now you can understand why it is important to determine which particular meaning of a word is being used in a given passage. How can we figure that out? Here are some practical steps to consider when interpreting words.

Choose a Balanced Bible Translation

There are three basic philosophies of Bible translation and I will illustrate each with a popular contemporary version of Scripture. At one end of the spectrum are the renditions that pride themselves on being *word-for-word* translations of the original languages. This very literal approach is best represented today by the English Standard Version (ESV). The publisher of this translation is an acquaintance of mine and an extremely generous man. He recently gave me a calfskin-covered copy of the *ESV Study Bible* that's worth hundreds of dollars. So, I would be ungrateful not to speak highly of the ESV. I mean, what's not to like about it?! Seriously, gift or not, the English Standard Version is an example of an effective word-for-word translation.

A word-for-word translation (the *King James Version* and *New American Standard Bible* are also representatives of this approach) is extremely helpful when doing in-depth Bible study that focuses on tracing certain words throughout Scripture. However, a word-for-word approach occasionally sacrifices something by way of readability. At times the text can be a bit stilted or wooden because of the effort to match every Hebrew and Greek word with a corresponding English word.

Perhaps an illustration totally unrelated to Bible translation would help here. Several years ago, Sue and I were eating out at a Mexican restaurant. This was a very authentic place, and we overheard a lot of Spanish being spoken around us. After our meal was served, a guy in a sombrero stopped by our table to serenade us with his guitar. The first verse of his song was sung in Spanish. Then he stumbled through a second verse in somewhat broken English. No doubt the translation was his own, as he warbled that his love was coming from "the bottom of my gut." *Gut* was probably a literal and accurate rendering of the Spanish at that point. But it didn't quite convey the same sentiment in English.

Word-for-word Bible translations, similarly, can sometimes leave us with an English version that is less than a smooth read. But perhaps this is just a matter of taste. Go ahead and take a look at the ESV for yourself. You may love it.

At the opposite end of the continuum from literal translations are the paraphrases. Instead of attempting a word-for-word correspondence between the biblical languages and English, paraphrases (sometimes called *free* translations) endeavor to make a *thought-for-thought* transference from the original language. The most popular representative of this approach today is probably Eugene Peterson's *The Message.* (Many Bible scholars would say that the *New Living Translation* is also a paraphrase. But its publisher rejects such a categorization, declaring it to be a *translation* by its very title.)

While paraphrases provide us with an easier-to-read text and minimize the cultural differences between the Bible's world and ours, they tend to sacrifice something by way of accuracy. And they don't make for good study Bibles, because they're not as concerned with translating *words* with consistency as they are with translating *ideas.*

The New International Version (NIV) represents a translation philosophy that stands midway between the literal (word-for-word) and the paraphrase (thought-for-thought) approaches. Bible scholars refer to it as a *dynamic equivalent* rendition. That is, it attempts to "translate words, idioms and grammatical constructions of the original language into precise equivalents in the receptor [i.e., English] language"—so says New Testament scholar Gordon Fee.[3] Dr. Fee declares this to be the best translational theory. And I tend to agree with him. The NIV combines a literal translation's emphasis on accuracy with a paraphrase's strength of readability.

Whatever Bible translation you choose to use (and I'm not shy about recommending the NIV, with my second favorite being the ESV), let me encourage you to stick with it for the long haul. Feel free to consult other versions when studying a passage. But choosing to "own" one as your primary version will result in a greater familiarity with the text over time. It will also encourage your memorization of Scripture.

Note: The publisher of the NIV recently updated its translation (2011). I must tell you, however, that I'm a fan of the older edition (1984) and don't care for many of the changes made to "improve" it.[4] Hasn't the NIV publisher heard of the debacle created by Coke some years ago when they tried to make us swallow a new recipe for our favorite cola? We rebelled and the soda maker gave us back our original drink as Coke Classic. How 'bout we all demand an NIV Classic? Just a thought, but we'll probably have to bite the bullet and make a transition to the new NIV.

Focus on Interpreting the Most Significant Words

Because the Bible declares itself to be inspired ("God-breathed"; 2 Timothy 3:16), it follows that all its words are inspired. So a word study of a key phrase is often helpful. You don't need to ruminate, however, on every use of "the" or "tree" or "go" in the text. Just look for the key nouns, verbs, and adjectives that seem to be crucial to the passage. Look for important words. Note, too, repeating words. If the same word is used several times within a few verses, it may indicate a theme that God wants to draw your attention to. You may also want to focus on words that are unclear or puzzling to you.

Let's say that you're reading in the second chapter of John's first epistle, and you come to verse 15: "Do not love the world or anything in the world. If anyone loves the world, the love of the Father is not in him." One of the significant words in this verse is certainly *world*—first, because it's repeated three times, and second, because it's a bit puzzling. Why puzzling? Well, doesn't this verse seem to be at odds with the most familiar verse in the Bible, also written by the apostle John? John 3:16 tells us: "God so loved the world that he gave his one and only Son." Yet 1 John 2:15 commands us: "Do not love the world." So, *God* loves the world but *we* shouldn't? Don't you find that puzzling?

IF WE PAY some attention to the word *world* we can deduce that John is using it in two different ways.

The apparent conflict between these two verses is easily resolved once we pay some attention to the word *world* and deduce that John is using it in two different ways. What does *world* mean in each of these two immediate settings?

World in John 3:16 is a reference to people in general. God loved humanity so much that He gave us His Son. But *world* in 1 John 2:15 is a reference to anti-God behaviors and attitudes held by the surrounding culture. How do we know that? Keep reading. The very next verse says: "For everything in the world—the cravings of sinful man, the lust of his eyes and the boasting of what he has and does—comes not from the Father but from the world" (1 John 2:16). So loving the *world* of people is a good thing, while loving the *world* of sin is not. Do you see the benefit of considering a word's immediate setting?

Avoid Faulty Interpretive Approaches

Some preachers (including me, on occasion) love to expound on particular words in the text that they've chosen for their sermon. The minute they say, "The Hebrew (or Greek) for this word is actually . . ." their listeners are wowed. It's assumed that what is said next will be deep and scholarly. But not every approach to interpreting words is helpful. In fact, some of the common approaches can be downright misleading. Watch out for four approaches.

First, putting too much emphasis on individual words. I know, here I've been promoting the study of words while reading the Bible, and now I'm going to tell you not to overdo that sort of thing! Let me explain by citing a passage that far too many preachers have misinterpreted because of their overemphasis on a distinction between two words.

In John 21:15–17, Jesus is having a postresurrection conversation with Peter. Three times Jesus asks Peter, "Do you love me?" The first couple of times Jesus asks the question, the Greek word He uses for love is *agapao.* But Peter uses a different Greek word for love, *phileo,* when he responds, "Lord, you know that I love you." So, the third time Jesus asks the question, he switches to Peter's word: "Do you love [*phileo,* not *agapao*] me?"

Some preachers (and Christian authors) have made a big deal of a supposed distinction between these two words, suggesting that the former (*agapao*) is a reference to divine love, while the latter (*phileo*) connotes human love or friendship. From this distinction they then sermonize that Jesus was hoping for some divinely inspired love (*agapao*) from Peter, but He eventually had to lower the bar and settle for Peter's human affection (*phileo*).

Unfortunately, a more extensive survey of these two Greek words for love indicates that they are not quite so distinct from one another in meaning. In fact, God the Father even uses *phileo* to speak of His love for His Son (John 5:20)! Of course, you're probably wondering how you could be expected to catch stuff like that. Do you have to know the biblical languages or conduct exhaustive searches of every significant word to make sure that preachers and authors aren't exaggerating their meaning?

No. Just be a bit suspicious when too much emphasis is placed on particular words. In the case of *agapao* versus *phileo* in John 21, it's simply not reasonable to conclude that the proper understanding of this passage should come down to our ability to distinguish between two Greek verbs that are both translated into English as *love*. Surely a correct interpretation will not depend on catching something so subtle.

Second, *relying on the etymology of words. Etymology* is just a fancy way of referring to a word's history. It sounds scholarly to hear someone describe what a Bible word originally meant, but that sort of an allusion can be terribly misleading. That's *not* how we discover what a word means in its immediate setting.

Let me illustrate why the etymology approach is faulty. Suppose you and I are sitting on a bench at the mall and you say, "Look at that cute girl." I pull out my iPad, do a quick Google search of the word *cute*, and learn that in Elizabethan England it meant *bowlegged*. (I'm not making this up.) Should I be scanning the crowd for a girl who looks like she just got off a horse? Of course not! The etymology of *cute* does not help me understand what you meant by it.

Dr. Grant Osborne, who's written a comprehensive book on hermeneutics, says: "Words are not used according to their historical value." It's unrealistic, he adds, to suppose that Bible authors would have in mind the semantic evolutions through which words have passed when selecting such words for their writings. "Words always have a current value," Osborne concludes, "limited to the moment when they're employed."[5] How words have been used in the past may give us some clues to their meaning, but how they are being used in the passage where we find them is what's most important.

Third, *taking apart compound words.* Once again, this is a favorite device of some preachers. They announce that a certain word in the text is a *compound word*, and then they proceed to break it down into its parts and define each part. Try doing that with an English compound word and see where it gets you. What about *butterfly*? Well, *butter* is the product of churned milk, and *fly* is the activity of sailing through the air. So, a *butterfly* must be a soaring lump of lard, right? The same sorts of misinterpretations will ensue if we break down the compound words *broadcast* or *hamburger* or *fellowship*.

However, lest we throw the baby out with the bathwater, it must be admitted that on occasion we may be able to learn something about the meaning of a compound word by dissecting it. A *houseboat*, for example, is a residence that floats on water. Similarly, the Greek New Testament word for church—*ekklesia*—aptly describes a group of people who have been called (*klesia*) out of (*ek*) the world to follow Christ.

So it's occasionally insightful to discover what each of the component parts of a compound word in the Bible means. But it would be dangerous to apply this method uncritically, especially if the rendered meaning is not supported by the immediate setting.

Fourth, *using multiple meanings for words*. Now that you know that many Bible words have multiple meanings, it may be tempting to ascribe significance to every definition of whatever word you choose to focus on in a passage. But you don't need to pay attention to multiple definitions of a word that you are studying. Simply select the single definition that fits its setting best. (In other words, *more* is not *better.*)

Moises Silva illustrates this point in his book on hermeneutics by asking us to imagine a foreign visitor who has just heard his American friend complain of an acute pain in her knee. The overseas guest wants to know what is meant by *acute.* Would the following response be helpful?

> In geometry, the word is used of angles less than 90 degrees, while in music it many indicate a high-pitched sound. It also is used to describe an accent mark in some languages and scripts. In objects it indicates a sharp point. The word can be used as a synonym for "keen, discerning, shrewd." Things of great importance can be said to be acute. In medicine, it may describe a disease that is approaching a crisis. Finally, the word can mean "severe."[6]

You may be wondering why I even bother to make this point. It's obviously absurd to latch onto every possible meaning of a word that you are studying in a passage. Of course you would select the single definition that best fits the context. Who couldn't figure this one out? Well, evidently the folks behind *The Amplified Bible* haven't figured it out. Here's how John 3:16 reads in the Amplified version: "For God so greatly loved and dearly prized the world that He [even] gave up His only begotten [unique] Son, so that whoever believes in (trusts in, clings to, relies on) Him shall not perish (come to destruction, be lost) but have eternal (everlasting) life."

This approach to Bible translation is almost humorous. Let me say (tell, declare, affirm) that this is no way (manner, form, custom) to communicate (correspond, talk, signal, disseminate information). Not only does such complexity make the text difficult to read, it also subtly suggests that when we come across a significant word in our Bible reading, we are free to choose whatever definition we like the most from a handful of possibilities. No! We must look for the single definition that is best suited to the context.

Enough about faulty approaches to be avoided. Here's a fifth *positive* rule for interpreting words accurately:

Interpret Words in Light of How They Are Used in Sentences, Paragraphs, Books, and the Bible as a Whole

This is the word's most *immediate setting* and often provides the best help you'll need for determining the meaning of that word. Moving out from the bull's-eye, the next ring represents the paragraph (or cluster of paragraphs) in which the sentence appears that contains your word. What is the gist of that paragraph and how does your word fit into it?

Once you understand how a word functions within its immediate paragraph, you can broaden your investigation of its meaning by examining how it's used elsewhere in the same Bible book. After that, the next step is to study its import in other books by the same author. Keep in mind that Moses wrote five books, Solomon three, Luke two, Paul thirteen, John five, and Peter two (plus an assist on the gospel of Mark). The assumption is that an author will use a word consistently within his own writings—but in a way that may differ from how others use that word.

The final setting in which to consider a word is the Bible as a whole. The fact that there is one divine Author behind the entire Book suggests that there will be some degree of consistency in what words mean throughout Scripture, even though each human author will have his own distinct vocabulary. The tool that will be most helpful in carrying out your contextual study of a word is the concordance at the back of your Bible. As I explained in the last chapter, a concordance lists alphabetically the most common words in the Bible with their Scriptures.

A Study of the Word *Yeast*

Are you ready to put into practice what you've just learned? Let's see how it works with a couple of words. We'll start with what appears to be a fairly straightforward word: *yeast*.

What does *yeast* mean? I'm sure that your quick response

is to identify yeast as the ingredient in bread dough that makes it rise. And that's exactly how Moses used the word when giving the Israelites instructions about Passover preparations: "For seven days you are to eat bread made without yeast" (Exodus 12:15).

But does it seem likely that Jesus has the literal meaning of *yeast* in mind when He warns His disciples, "Be on your guard against the yeast of the Pharisees" (Luke 12:1)? Hardly! Jesus was not conducting a cooking class for His followers. So what did He mean by His use of the word *yeast*? Fortunately, Jesus Himself defines the word at the sentence's end: "Be on your guard against the yeast of the Pharisees, which is hypocrisy." Hypocrisy is a two-faced behavior that can permeate a person's character like yeast working its way through a lump of dough.

This negative meaning of yeast, however, could not be what Jesus had in mind on another occasion when He used the word to describe the kingdom of God.

Then Jesus asked, "What is the kingdom of God like? What shall I compare it to? It is like a mustard seed, which a man took and planted in his garden. It grew and became a tree, and the birds of the air perched in its branches."

Again he asked, "What shall I compare the kingdom

of God to? It is like yeast that a woman took and mixed into a large amount of flour until it worked all through the dough." (Luke 13:18–21)

Doesn't it help to look at the entire paragraph here to determine how Jesus is using the word *yeast*? The kingdom of God is spreading, just as yeast spreads through dough. And in case we might miss the analogy, Jesus precedes it with a description of a mustard seed growing into a tree. Same idea, confirming our understanding of *yeast*: God's kingdom is getting bigger and bigger.

But sometimes even the immediate paragraph is no help when interpreting a word. This is the case when Jesus cautions His disciples: "Be on your guard against the yeast of the Pharisees and Sadducees" (Matthew 16:6). At first glance, this seems like a repeat of the Luke 12:1 warning to steer clear of hypocrisy. But *yeast* isn't identified as hypocrisy on this occasion. In fact, *yeast* isn't identified at all, leaving the disciples to speculate about what Jesus means. They initially conclude that He must be using the word literally—Jesus is chiding them for forgetting to bring bread on their outing across the lake (v. 5). They must be at fault for having nothing to eat.

But this is not what Jesus means by *yeast* in this setting. We have to keep on reading if we want to find out what He has in mind. After He reminds His disciples that on two previous occasions He had fed thousands of people with only a few loaves of bread, they realize that *yeast* couldn't possibly be a reference to Jesus' concern that they lacked bread. The lightbulbs begin to go on. Jesus is using the word metaphorically. "Then they understood that he was not telling them to guard against the yeast used in bread, but against the teaching of the Pharisees and Sadducees" (Matthew 16:12). So *yeast* means false teaching in this passage—a definition only arrived at after reading a couple paragraphs of text (vv. 7–12).

Now that we've looked at a few instances where Jesus used the word *yeast*, let's see what Paul does with it. In 1 Corinthians 5:6–7, Paul writes: "Your boasting is not good. Don't you know that a little yeast works through the whole batch of dough? Get rid of the old yeast that you may be a new batch without yeast." What is the *old yeast* that Paul wants the Corinthians to get rid of? We won't find an answer to that question in the sentence that the word appears in. Nor in the surrounding paragraph.

If we want to find out what Paul means by *old yeast* we need to read the entire chapter of 1 Corinthians 5. Here's the skinny: sexual immorality is rampant in Corinth—and not just in the city, but in the local church. The worst case is that of a guy who's sleeping with his stepmom! Paul tells these believers to kick this guy out of their congregation if he's not willing to repent of his sin. Otherwise, his promiscuous behavior will spread to others. Getting rid of the old yeast is finally spelled out near the close of the chapter with these words: "You must not associate with anyone who calls himself a brother but is sexually immoral" (1 Corinthians 5:11). So *yeast* in this case refers to a professing Christ follower who is unrepentantly engaged in flagrant sin.

One final example, also from Paul, of the use of *yeast*:

> You were running a good race. Who cut in on you and kept you from obeying the truth? That kind of persuasion does not come from the one who calls you. "A little yeast works through the whole batch of dough." I am confident in the Lord that you will take no other view. The one who is throwing you into confusion will pay the penalty, whoever he may be. Brothers, if I am still preaching circumcision, why am I still being persecuted? In that case the offense of the cross has been abolished. As for those agitators, I wish they would go the whole way and emasculate themselves! (Galatians 5:7–12)

Paul's concern, expressed in these verses, is that the Christ followers in Galatia are allowing certain false doctrines to lead them away from the truth that he had preached to them. This heresy (and the people who promoted it) is the *yeast* that Paul warns them against. What exactly does this dangerous teaching consist of? You can pick up a hint of it in this paragraph. It's got something to do with an emphasis on the Jewish ritual of circumcision. But if this paragraph were all you had to go on, you would be somewhat in the dark with regard to all Paul means by *yeast* in this setting.

So, what do you do? You sit down and read through the six short chapters of Galatians. Don't forget to start with the one-page introduction to this epistle that you'll find in your study Bible. By the time you're finished with Galatians (thirty minutes, tops), you'll have a thorough understanding of the heresy of the *Judaizers*, who taught that faith in Christ is not enough for salvation. Faith must be accompanied by good works—especially certain Jewish rituals. This is the *yeast* that Paul did not want permeating the church in Galatia.

We're done with our survey of the word *yeast*. It's used in a wide variety of ways in the Bible. You've seen how its meaning sometimes lies on the surface (i.e., the actual ingredient in bread dough, Exodus 12:15). But on other occasions, we couldn't discover the word's meaning until we searched the host sentence (hypocrisy, Luke 12:1); or the surrounding paragraph (the kingdom of God, Luke 13:18–21), or a cluster of several paragraphs (false teaching, Matthew 6:6–12); or an entire chapter (sexual immorality, 1 Corinthians 5); or a complete book of the Bible (the Judaizers' heresy, Galatians).

A Study of the Word *Justify*

Allow me to give you a second example of researching a word's meaning in its immediate sentence, then paragraph(s), then book of the Bible, and then Bible as a whole. We will study a key verb in the Bible: *justify*.

I promise not to take as much time with this word as I did with *yeast*. But it *is* one of the most important words in the Bible! The reason I've chosen this word is because a failure to correctly interpret what it means in its specific context could result in a misunderstanding of how a person is able to experience God's salvation.

LET'S PIT Paul's use of *justify* in Romans 3:28 against that of James in James 2:24. Could any two statements be more at odds with each other?

Let's jump right into the thick of it. I'm going to pit Paul's use of *justify* against that of James. In Romans 3:28, Paul writes: "For we maintain that a man is justified by faith apart from observing the law." Contrast that with James 2:24: "You see that a person is justified by what he does and not by faith alone." Could any two statements be more at odds with each other than these?

One conclusion we might be tempted to draw from this comparison is that the Bible contradicts itself. Paul, the author of thirteen Bible epistles, says that justification is the result of faith *plus nothing*. James, also the author of a Bible epistle, says that it is the result of faith *plus works*. So it seems that the Bible occasionally disagrees with the Bible. However, we've previously concluded that this can never be the case, since the Bible is ultimately the product of the same Divine Mind: God's! God is not going to disagree with Himself.

The only other conclusion we can draw from this seemingly major rift between Paul and James is that they're talking about two different matters. Proving this conclusion looks, initially, like an uphill battle, not only because both writers use the same key word (*justify*), but also because they use the same Bible character (Abraham) to illustrate what they mean by the word. It doesn't look like they're talking about two different matters. It looks like they're talking about the same thing and spouting contradictory viewpoints!

But when we take a closer look at the paragraphs around Romans 3:28 and James 2:24, we see signs that Paul and James are addressing two different issues. Even in their citing of Abraham as a role model they draw from two separate incidents in this great patriarch's life. (See Romans 4:9–25 and James 2:20–23.) Paul recalls how Abraham, though he was advanced in years, believed in God's promise of a son. It was on the basis of this faith that God justified him. James, on the other hand, references Abraham's willingness to offer up that son, Isaac, years later on an altar. It was by this action, James says, that Abraham was justified.

These two events in Abraham's life tip us off that Paul and James are making completely different points. Paul is concerned with how we begin a relationship with God. There's nothing we can do to earn this status. We must put our faith in God's promised Son—not Isaac, but Jesus. When we do that, God *declares* us to be righteous in His sight based upon the forgiveness which Christ purchased for us on the cross.

In contrast, James is concerned with what we do *after* we decide to put our trust in Christ. How can we be sure that our faith is the real deal? Abraham demonstrated the genuineness of his faith in God by a willingness to sacrifice his son, Isaac, as God had commanded. Are our lives producing a similar obedience that confirms an authentic faith in Christ?

So when Paul speaks of what it means to be justified, he has in mind *God's declaration* of our righteousness, which is based solely on our faith in Jesus Christ. But when James speaks of what it means to be justified, he has in mind *our demonstration* of righteousness, which will result from a true faith in Jesus Christ. So Romans 3:28 and James 2:24 are not contradictory, they're complementary. And the only way to figure that out is by studying *justify* in the immediate contexts of Paul's and James's epistles.

Our surveys of the Bible's use of *yeast* and *justify* have underscored how important it is to interpret the meaning of individual words with respect to their immediate setting. How do they fit into their sentence, paragraph (and surrounding paragraphs), book, and the Bible as a whole? This question should also be asked when we are seeking to interpret concepts that are expressed by groups of words. In order to ascertain whether we correctly understand these concepts, we must take a closer look at the immediate settings in which they appear. Let's do that with a couple of examples.

A Closer Look at Two Phrases

Jesus taught His disciples, "For where two or three come together in my name, there am I with them" (Matthew 18:20). Some have interpreted this statement to be the simplest definition of a church. What constitutes a church? All it takes, they say, is for two or three believers to be in the same place at the same time.

One popular Christian pollster even cites this passage to suggest that we need a revolution in how we do church today. It's time, he says, for us to give up our outdated notion of the local church, with its worship services, Bible studies, and ministries. Local churches are now passé. As we head into the future, the church will exist wherever two or three Christ followers are hanging out together. According to this pollster's definition, even a couple of buddies playing golf on a Sunday morning would qualify as a church.[7]

But before you abandon your local church for eighteen holes with a friend next weekend, let me push back on this interpretation of Matthew 18:20. If your Bible is handy, open it and turn to the verse. It serves as a wrap-up to a lesson that began in verse 15. What's the topic of the lesson? The paragraph heading in my Bible reads: "A Brother Who Sins Against You." Jesus is teaching about how to resolve a conflict with someone who wrongs you. The first thing you do is go to him privately and discuss the problem. If that doesn't work, you return with a friend to back you up. And if the offender still stubbornly resists your attempt to reconcile with him, get the *church* (presumably a few leaders) involved.

This is the point at which Jesus makes the statement about two or three gathering in His name. He's not explaining to us what constitutes a church. He's not talking about getting together for worship services—or golf. He's laying out a strategy for resolving conflict. Do you see how important it is to check out the *immediate context* of a concept that you encounter in Scripture?

Here's a second phrase: "One will be taken and the other left." This phrase appears twice in a lesson that Jesus taught about His future return. Jesus describes a coming day when two men will be working in a field and one will be taken and the other left. The same thing will happen to two women who are grinding away with a hand mill (Matthew 24:40–

41). What event does Jesus have in mind here? Some say that this is a vivid description of the rapture—that secret coming of Christ, when He whisks believers off the planet before the Great Tribulation strikes. Jesus' full return to earth, they say, will occur visibly and gloriously seven years later. So, those *taken* in the Matthew account are raptured Christ followers.

This interpretation became so popular in the early 1970s that pioneer Christian rocker Larry Norman wrote a song based on it, "I Wish We'd All Been Ready." (DC Talk later did a retro version of the tune.) The lyrics warn us about the following scenario:

> "Two men walking up a hill,
> one disappears and one's left standing still,
> I wish we'd all been ready.
> There's no time to change your mind,
> the Son has come and you've been left behind."[8]

This song is near and dear to my heart, because I was a high school student when it hit the charts. So, I chose to sing it as a duet with a friend of mine at our public high school's annual talent show. This led to my being "discovered" by the choir director, followed by a couple years of fame (OK, I'm slightly exaggerating) in various school musical performances. But on a more serious note (awful pun), this song reflects what I would argue is a misinterpretation of Matthew 24.

Take a look at the immediate context of the line: "one will be taken and the other left." Just before Jesus describes one of two men being taken from a field and one of two women being taken from the mill, he references the story of Noah: "For in the days before the flood, people were eating and drinking, marrying and giving in marriage, up to the day Noah entered the ark; and they knew nothing about what would happen until the flood came and took them all away" (Matthew 24:38–39).

What people are described by the phrase *took them all away* in this account? Noah and his family—who were carried to safety by the ark? No, this is a reference to the wicked people who were *taken away* in judgment by the flood.

So, when Jesus speaks, in the very next verses, about a man who is *taken* from a field and a woman who is *taken* from her mill, He is not alluding to believers who will be raptured [taken away] from the earth to safety before the Great Tribulation begins. Jesus is talking about those who will be *taken* in judgment from the earth when He returns to set up His kingdom. The fact that Jesus goes on to warn His listeners about this judgment in the rest of Matthew 24 seems to confirm this interpretation. "One will be taken and the other left" does not support the notion of a rapture. Those who adopt the concept of a return of Christ to rapture believers into heaven seem to be ignoring the immediate setting.

Now would be a good time to summarize what I've been emphasizing in this chapter with a pithy saying that I heard years ago: "A text without a context becomes a proof text for a pretext." Did you follow that? If a word or concept that we read in the Bible (*text*) is interpreted without reference to its host sentence, paragraph(s), book, and Bible (*context*), we may mistakenly think we've found evidence (*proof text*) for our preconceived beliefs (*pretext*).

You must understand the context! When interpreting the Bible, this means that it is critical to consider the historical, literary, theological, and immediate settings of every passage we read. And now that you've grasped the importance of *context*, you're ready to move on to applying the Bible to your daily life. *Walk* (book four in the Bible Savvy series) will equip you to do this.

Study Guide
The Immediate Context

Icebreaker

How many different meanings for the word "run" can you come up with?

1. Explain the three translation philosophies behind the various Bible versions.

What is the Bible translation that you most often use? Why? Which category of translation philosophy does it fall into? What are the strengths and weaknesses of such a translation?

2. 🗨 If you want to interpret the Bible correctly, you must learn to recognize key words as you read. Take a look at the following passages and note the most significant word(s) or phrase(s) in each:

Genesis 45:3–9 (this one is so obvious you might miss it, but you can check your answer by comparing it to what you find in Genesis 50:20)

Deuteronomy 28:1–14

Ezekiel 33:1–9

John 15:1–8

1 Corinthians 9:19–23

Hebrews 9:11–14

3. *The Amplified Bible* is constructed on what premise? What is the weakness of such a premise?

4. Read Joshua 1. What command does God repeatedly give Joshua? From the context of this chapter, how does a person come by these two characteristics?

5. 🗣 The opening declaration of Jesus' ministry, recorded in Mark 1:15, is: "The time has come. The kingdom of God is near. Repent and believe the good news!" If the kingdom of God was the first thing out of Jesus' mouth, this must be a very important biblical topic. Using your concordance, briefly summarize what the gospel of Mark teaches about this subject.

🗣 Based upon what you have learned about the kingdom of God in Mark, is this a present or a future reality? Explain. (The *NIV Study Bible* has an extremely helpful footnote along these lines for Luke 4:43.) What bearing does this have on your life today?

6. In Matthew 5:14, Jesus announces to His followers, "You are the light of the world." But this verse doesn't say what is meant by that metaphor. You'll need to look at a wider context to discover what it means to be *light*. How would you define being *the light of the world* according to the context of:

   a. the Matthew 5:14–16 paragraph?

   b. Jesus' Sermon on the Mount in Matthew 5–7 (cite broad categories)?

   c. other New Testament writers in 2 Corinthians 4:5–7; Ephesians 5:8–13; 1 Peter 2:9; 1 John 1:5–9; 2:9–10?

7. The apostle Paul seems to express a negative viewpoint toward God's law in Romans 7, noting that Christ followers have both "died to the law" (7:4) and been "released from the law" (7:6). This has led some believers to conclude that God's law has no relevance for their lives today. But read Romans 7 in its entirety and sum up this chapter's *balanced* perspective on God's law.

This same balanced perspective can be seen in the broader context of the epistle of Romans. Note what Paul says, positively and negatively, about the law in Romans 3:20, 31.

Evidently, there is a very specific sense in which Christ followers are to see themselves as released from the law. In what sense is it no longer applicable to you? In what sense does the law still have a role to play in your life?

What additional positive remarks do other Bible writers make about God's law—most notably, the psalmist (Psalm 119:1, 18, 44–45, 52, 62, 72, 92, 97–98, 136, 156, 165) and two of the major prophets (Jeremiah 31:33; Ezekiel 36:26–27)?

8. *Cessationists* believe that the biblical gift of tongues is no longer given to believers by the Holy Spirit today. A key text that is used to support this position is 1 Corinthians 13:8: "Where there are tongues, they will be stilled." Cessationists say that the apostle Paul is looking to his near future when the New Testament canon would be completed and there would no longer be a need for revelation from God through tongues.

Read 1 Corinthians 13:8–12. What time frame does this context suggest for when tongues would be stilled? Explain.

Now read the context of the following chapter, 1 Corinthians 14. Is there any mention of the cessation of tongues in this passage? What *does* Paul say about tongues by way of guidelines for using this gift?

Notes

About the Bible Savvy Series

1. Thom S. Rainer, *The Unchurched Next Door* (Grand Rapids: Zondervan, 2003), 200.

Chapter 1: The Historical Setting

1. R. C. Sproul, *Knowing Scripture* (Downers Grove, Ill.: InterVarsity, 1977), 64.

Chapter 3: The Theological Setting

1. Legally, Kody Brown has a civil marriage with one of the four women; he calls the other three "sister wives." When Utah law enforcement officials began investigating whether Brown had violated state law banning polygamy, the Browns threated a lawsuit to challenge the polygamy law. Charges were later dropped. See John Schwartz, "Polygamist, Under Scrutiny in Utah, Plans Suit to Challenge Law," *New York Times*, July 11, 2011; "Polygamy Charges Against Sister Wives' Kody Brown Dropped," *US Weekly*, June 1, 2012.

2. See http://hollywoodlife.com/celeb/kody-brown.

3. If you too aspire to be a better pray-er, I recommend James L. Nicodem, *Prayer Coach* (Wheaton: Crossway, 2008).

Chapter 4: The Immediate Setting

1. From Kip Wheeler, "Reasons Why the English Language Is Hard to Learn," http://web.cn.edu/kwheeler/English_hard_2learn.html. Dr. Wheeler, an associate professor of English at Carson-Newman University in Jefferson City, Tennessee, compiled his listing from various articles by Richard Lederer and the anonymous poem "The English Lesson."

2. J. Scott Duvall and J. Daniel Hays, *Grasping God's Word* (Grand Rapids: Zondervan, 2001).

3. Gordon D. Fee and Douglas Stuart, *How to Read the Bible for All Its Worth* (Grand Rapids: Zondervan, 2003), 35.

4. For example, I read the famous Shepherd Psalm in the new translation and saw that they had changed "the valley of the shadow of death" to "the darkest valley" (Psalm 23:4). *Are you kidding me? Nixing "the valley of the shadow of death"? There are some things you just don't mess with!* And the use of "they" and "them" plural pronouns linked to singular verbs when referring to either sex at times sounds strange to me.

5. Grant Osborne, *The Hermeneutical Spiral*, rev. ed. (Downers Grove, Ill.: InterVarsity, 2006), 70.

6. Moises Silva, *An Introduction to Biblical Hermeneutics* (Grand Rapids: Zondervan, 2007), 58.

7. George Barna, *Revolution* (Carol Stream, Ill.: Tyndale, 2006), 1–2, chapter 7. For a critique of the book, see Kevin Miller, "No Church? No Problem," http://www.christianity today.com/ct/2006/january/13.69.html.

8. Larry Norman, "I Wish We'd All Been Ready," copyright 1969 by Larry Norman. Used by permission of the Larry Norman Trust. All rights reserved.

Bibliography

Driscoll, Mark and Gerry Breshears. *Doctrine: What Christians Should Believe*. Wheaton: Crossway, 2010.

Duvall, J. Scott and J. Daniel Hays. *Grasping God's Word: A Hands-On Approach to Reading, Interpreting, and Applying the Bible*. Grand Rapids: Zondervan, 2005.

ESV Study Bible. Wheaton: Crossway, 2008. Print.

Fee, Gordon D. and Douglas Stuart. *How to Read the Bible for All Its Worth*. Grand Rapids: Zondervan, 2003.

Grudem, Wayne. *Systematic Theology*. Grand Rapids: Zondervan, 1994.

NIV Study Bible. Grand Rapids: Zondervan, 2008. Print.

Osborne, Grant. *The Hermeneutical Spiral: A Comprehensive Introduction to Biblical Interpretation*, rev. ed. Downers Grove, Ill.: InterVarsity, 2006.

JAMES L. NICODEM

Bible Savvy

Epic: The Storyline of the Bible unveils the single theme that ties all of scripture together: redemption.

Foundation: The Trustworthiness of the Bible explains where our current bible came from and why it can be wholly trusted.

Context: How to Understand the Bible shows readers how to read the different parts of the Bible as they were meant to be read and how they fit together.

Walk: How to Apply the Bible puts the readers increased understanding of the Bible into real life terms and contexts.

COMA

Passage
- Themes
- Repetitive Words
- Truths about God
- Striking Something